D1441064

The CRAFT and the MAKERS

TRADITION WITH ATTITUDE

Edited by Duncan Campbell, Charlotte Rey,

Sven Ehmann, and Robert Klanten

gestalten

Contents

Introduction

When we were approached to work on this book, we wanted to explore the value of craftsmanship in the context of contemporary society. It's a subject that has long fascinated us and influenced our work, particularly with a view to the dedication needed to master a particular craft, and a love of the unique and beautiful products that skilled craftspeople produce. In an industrialized civilization that relies increasingly on automated production processes, it felt important to reassert the significance of things made with passion and dexterity by human hands.

It hardly needs to be said that the subject of crafts is vast. Countless books have been written by those far more qualified than ourselves on the minutiae of a particular era of Japanese ceramic manufacture or English silversmithing. Safe in the knowledge that this could never be an exhaustive directory of contemporary craftspeople, nor a forensic exploration of a single technique, material or trade, the intention was to take a snapshot, a cross-section of makers currently working around the world. As this is a book on craftsmanship in a broad sense, and not on a single craft, we will present a wide variety of different crafts, some of which may seem obvious while others are perhaps rather controversial, but we feel that each featured maker is special in their own way, and that the accompanying imagery speaks for itself.

It struck us that the perception of the word craft had perhaps changed in recent years. Just as the word luxury has lost its lust, we wondered if the notion of craft itself had become somehow tainted—perceived as frivolous, unnecessary, or inferior. It's not our job to comment on the validity of one type of craft over another, but we did know the spirit that we wanted to celebrate in this book. We wanted to think about craft that had a purity of purpose, that melded tradition and innovation and that avoided both cozy nostalgia and newness for its own sake. It was important to look at a broad range of makers and crafts, from the rarefied, the luxurious, and the decorative to the practical and the utilitarian. What, we hope, unites everyone featured is both a dedication to their chosen vocation and the beauty and integrity of the final product.

Some craftspeople work by and for themselves, some have built multinational businesses, some work with materials in places that have for many centuries been synonymous with their trade, and some are still being challenged over whether what they do constitutes a craft at all. But from California to Tokyo, from Mali to the Arctic Circle, they are all united by the same unwavering dedication to excellence in what they produce and devotion to a lifetime of learning.

One thing that may be conspicuous in its absence is any mention of cost. This was a conscious decision, with the eminently quotable Oscar Wilde on particularly good form when he gave us this gem: "What is a cynic? A man who knows the price of everything and the value of nothing." We live in a time when the cost of everything is seen as a measure of its right to exist, and we wanted instead to consider craft in terms of its value. This could mean the value of personal relationships, the value in techniques saved from extinction, the value to a community centered around craft production, the value in hard work, the value in sourcing materials responsibly and the glorious reality that there are still some things money can't buy.

by Duncan Campbell and Charlotte Rey

The Essence of Craft

When one considers craft and craftspeople, it is easy to forget that the subject is not an industry in and of itself but rather represents the pinnacle of quality within many fields where human creativity and manufacturing meet. The institutional values of craft encompass excellence, the pushing of boundaries, and the ability to combine traditional knowledge with modern thinking in order to create something beautiful and unique, and this is something that today feels more relevant than ever. We live in a disposable society, obsessed with novelty and ease of consumption. Increasingly, work days are spent in front of a screen, and the notion of craft in the context of our daily lives represents a return to tactility, physicality, and the sense of something real. In recent years, craft has experienced a surge of renewed interest and this is due in part to the consumer's desire for products imbued with a human touch and a sense or permanence, rather than the standard uniformity of the production line. In addition, the question of provenance is becoming ever more important. Today an increased desire to know about the products we use, where they come from, who made them, and how far they have traveled are all questions that count in favor of the contemporary craftsman.

IKSEL DECORATIVE ARTS is a studio dedicated to painting and paneling for interior decoration, specializing in hand-painted and custom-printed wallpapers that bring an exotic, opulent, and elegant touch to their projects. Based between Paris and Istanbul with workshops of painters and draftsmen and women in Jaipur, India, it was founded in 1988 by husband-and-wife team Mehmet and Dimonah Iksel who met in Rajasthan on April, 1 of that year thanks to a flipped coin. Believing that certain avant-garde designs are too aggressive for the home, Mehmet and Dimonah prefer a gentler approach. The company stands firmly in the tradition of serene beauty in the decorative arts and offers wall decorations with a single scene or panoramas rather than repeated patterns. The designs often feature classical images like potted palms or landscapes in muted colors, botanicals, faux tapestries, chinoiseries, architectural elements or trompe l'oeil, often with a patina, and celebrating the European tradition of mixing styles and periods.

LAPICIDA, one of the world's leading natural stone specialists, was founded in 1984 by managing director Jason Cherrington. He recognized the potential after traveling to the Far East and bringing back some stone floor tile samples with him. Since then, the company has grown to become an international market leader with offices in New York, Mallorca, and Oslo as well as the headquarters in Harrogate, Yorkshire. The scope and visibility of stonemasonry has changed significantly over the last century. Once a common trade and much in demand, the advent of new construction techniques, increased reliance on technology, and a move to cheaper, more manageable building materials like glass and steel have led to a decline in the role of the traditional skilled stonemason. Lapicida (Latin for stoneworker) specializes in the highest quality stones

and marble from quarries around the world, including Carrara marble from Tuscany, famously the source for Michelangelo's *David.* Their work showcases the almost limitless potential of limestone, travertine, marble, onyx, slate, sandstone, rock crystal, and other semi-precious stones, and is used in everything from stone flooring and ornamentation to balustrades, statuary, and intricate mosaic work. Employing over 100 dedicated artisans at their Yorkshire site alone, the Lapicida craftsmen are some of the best in the world.

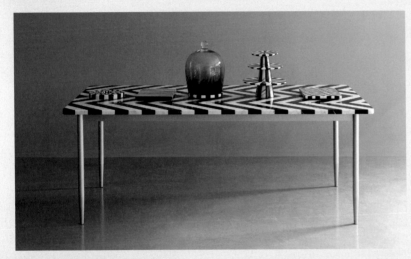

Officina Profumo Farmaceutica di SANTA MARIA NOVELLA, better known as Santa Maria Novella, is the oldest continuously operating pharmacy in the world. Located on Via della Scala in Florence, Dominican monks from the adjacent Basilica of Santa Maria Novella first established it in 1221 when they started growing herbs in their garden next to the monastery to make balms, elixirs, salves, ointments, liqueurs, and medicines for their infirmary. The pharmacy was renowned for its quality, and eventually became so popular that the monk Fra' Angiolo Marchissi, inspired by the laws of alchemy, opened the pharmacy for the public in 1612 with the blessing of His Highness the Grand Duke of Tuscany. Contemporary production takes place in the cellar laboratory in Via Reginaldo Guiliani, with various workshops for per-

fume and cosmetics. The formulas written down by the monks in ancient manuscripts and handed down through the centuries are still used today. In 2012, on the 400th anniversary of the business, Santa Maria Novella completely restored the historical building, a former papal residence, in Via della Scala to its original appearance with vaulted ceilings, ornate gilding, frescoes, walnut cabinetry, glass-stoppered decanters full of colorful potions, marble floors, glass-stained windows, bronze statues, and antique apothecary scales and mortars. •

The Craftsmen

The traditional image of an old man huddled over a workbench, while doubtless true to form in some instances, is by no means the whole story when talking about craftspeople in general. While there is no such thing as a typical craftsman, more often than not, they have dedicated themselves to a lifetime of learning—the considerable time it takes to acquire knowledge, gain experience, and to master their chosen crafts. In this way, contemporary craftspeople are as much a reflection of our modern society as the crafts themselves. The qualities that bring them together—a determined mindset, a dedication to excellence, a keen eye, and an artful touch—are, regardless of age, gender, or nationality, universal in their application. Whether leaders in their fields or apprentices just starting out, it is a sense of unwavering dedication to the honing and application of their crafts that unites them all. •

The Magic of Material and Techniques

Whether they start with something as humble and unadulterated as a piece of wood or as precious as a diamond, it is the notion of transformation during the process of crafting that defines each piece of a crafted product. The raw materials in the hands of a skilled artisan is where the true potential lies and is in part what makes the outcome so exciting. Thus, the sourcing of materials, whether it be clay from the peak of a Japanese mountain, rare foraged botanicals, or marble from an Italian quarry, is an essential part of the process. In many cases, these crafts have defined where a particular industry is based in the world with places like Grasse, Uji, and Florence being synonymous with the crafts on which the backbone of their existence is founded. The techniques of a craftsperson are like never-ending stories, with each individual bound to a lifetime chasing the next level of perfection, widening their horizons, pushing new boundaries, and improving on what went before.

KAIKADO OF KYOTO are the oldest makers of handmade, tin tea caddies in the world. The first generation began producing their innovative Chazutsu caddies in 1875 using sheets of tin specially imported from Cornwall with the English traders. Kaikado's iconic cylinder caddies quickly became the style of choice and were widely copied, but their quality was never equaled. The family's ancestors' caddies are still widely used across Japan and even found in the Japanese imperial household. Each caddy has two layers: an inner layer of tin, and an outer layer of tin, brass, copper, or silver depending on the design. The double wall of metal is perfect for storage, keeping the tins completely airtight and the contents dry. With daily use, the outer metal layer soon develops a unique patina that makes the caddy even more beautiful.

Founded as the KÖNIGLICH PRIVILEGIERTE THERESIENTHALER KRISTALLGLASFABRIK in 1836 by Franz and Wilhelm Steigerwald, the crystal maker has supplied Russian tsars and German kings with their handmade glasses, bowls, carafes, and tableware. Employing glassblowers, cutters, engravers, painters, and other craftsmen the crystal ware is made entirely by hand and their range of colored crystal is especially appreciated and collected worldwide. The process starts with the making of a wooden mold, which is carried out by a master woodturner. The

liquid glass is blown into the mold to form the cup, and a strand of molten glass is then formed into the stem that is attached to the cup before it solidifies. The glasses are then cut, engraved or painted, depending on the final designs, and polished by hand at the facility in Bavaria.

Universally recognized among the most renowned brands in Spain, LLADRÓ is an art porcelain maker based in Valencia. Standing for tradition, art, and prestige, three brothers Juan, José, and Vicente founded the company in 1953 when they began to fire their first creations in a Moorish kiln in their backyard. Now employing over 1,000 people, with stores in New York, Beverly Hills, Tokyo, London, and Shanghai amongst others, they are just as committed to their artisanal heritage. Each piece begins with a drawing, before it's modeled in clay or plasticine, and then divided into as many fragments as necessary for the work to be produced in porcelain. From each of the fragments, a mold is made and filled with liquid porcelain paste to create each element of the piece. Expert hands then put together the work using porcelain paste as an adhesive. •

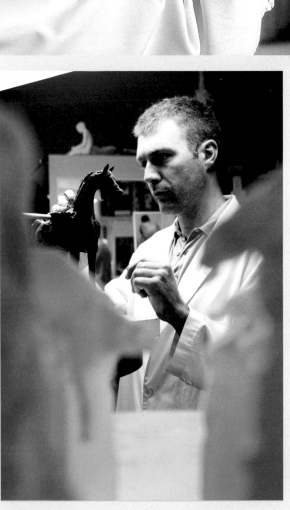

Workshops, Tools, and Factories

The spaces that craftspeople work in can themselves tell a thousand stories. Like the artist's studio, the craftsman's workshop and its tools are imbued with a certain kind of intangible magic. Whether it's a workshop occupied by the same family for a hundred years, an atelier linked to a specific geographical region or a gleaming factory restored to its former glory, each one is unique in its purpose and atmosphere. There are spaces with roaring furnaces, molten metal, and sparking machines just as others are so clinical, quiet, and precise that an observer could hear a pin drop onto the gleaming floor. Similarly, the tools used by each individual craftsperson, which over time often become like an extension of their hands, are suffused with personalities all of their own. Many of the tools haven't changed in form or application in many years, often having been passed down through generations and colored with a distinctive patina that only time and use can create. Heavy or light, hard or soft, from hammer to chisel and brush—they each have their own story to tell.

A lifelong motorcycle enthusiast and former member of a road racing team, WALT SIEGL trained as a toolmaker and welder in Germany, and it was only after he started to build motorcycles as a hobby that he considered turning it into a business. After moving to New York for a spell, he set up a full customization workshop in an old mill in Harrisville, New Hampshire in 2007. The unassuming space itself belies the beauty of the machines inside. Surfaces covered with oil-stained mechanic's tools, welding equipment, and angle grinders hint at the power and precision of his custom-built motorcycles which are some of the most sought after and technologically advanced in the United States.

MICHAEL RUH'S glass work embodies a subtle balance of color, texture, and form. After time spent traveling across the United States through arid deserts and over mountains, selling his work at art festivals, he eventually settled in South London to found his studio. It's the tones of the Midwestern sunsets and harvest landscapes he saw on his journey that inspire many of the color choices in his work today. His studio is a bright, inviting space in South London lined with huge windows where his small team works in the almost dance-like synchronization that glass production requires.

Born in 1972, RENÉ TALMON L'ARMÉE is a jewelry artisan who primarily works with natural colored and black diamonds, Tahitian black pearls and printed leather, combining them with precious stones, metals such as oxidized silver and 18-carat yellow gold. Joining the Berlin Werkstatt für Schmuckgestaltung in 1995, he went on to found his own atelier in 2001 in Paris after a stint in the Hermès workshops. In addition, he also works on a number of more fashion-forward, handmade lines, but he prefers bespoke orders, which he creates in his ateliers in Paris's Marais district and in Berlin's Mitte before his customers' eyes. His boutique workshops feature dark walls, reclaimed tile floors, antique vitrines, and beautiful furniture, amongst which are presented his jewelry collections alongside selected objets d'art. •

Art and Design

Simultaneously as we are experiencing a global resurgence of interest in the return to handmade, individual, and unique products, we are also in a new era of collaboration. The creative disciplines that were once distinct are becoming increasingly blurred, and interior designers and artists alike are turning to craft techniques in order to incorporate them into their practices in unusual and surprising ways. Additionally, artists are becoming more interested in executing their intricate conceptual ideas with a process that matches the elevation of their thought process. Often, these progressive thinkers face difficult obstacles finding facilities that are able to carry out their requests, and this is where collaborations with expert craftspeople come in. An individual dialogue can take place and develop a concept further as the artist's idea meets the hands and extensive knowledge of the craft worker. Also increasingly popular are collaborations between established houses and cutting-edge designers, who are given the opportunity to reinterpret the houses' archives or disrupt and advance their traditional working methods.

Born in Madrid 1974, artist-designer JAIME HAYON was included in *Time* magazine's list of the 100 most relevant creators of our time, with *Wallpaper** magazine naming him one of the most influential creators of the last decade. His prolific output blurs the lines between art, decoration, and design, spearheading a renaissance in intricate, finely crafted objects carefully presented within the cultural context of contemporary design. Jaime glides effortlessly between product, interior and furniture design, as well as sculpture and art installation. In his many exhibitions in galleries around the world, he often returns to his enthusiasm for preserving craft skills and merging them with his own practice, having collaborated with Baccarat, Lladró, Magis, Established & Sons, and Fabergé amongst others.

ELISA STROZYK was born in 1982 in Berlin and went on to do a Masters in Future Textile Design at London's Central Saint Martins. Winning the Salone del Mobile newcomer award Salone Satellite in 2011, she exhibits internationally with a progressive range of products from the deconstructed wooden carpet, made in conjunction with Böwer to her latest project, a collection of ceramic tables. Different liquid glazes mix and pool together while the tables are rotated and air blown to create fluid, smoke-like patterns which are then solidified under heat.

Both born in Tel Aviv in 1976, Yael Mer and Shay Alkalay obtained diplomas from the Royal College of Art in London in 2006, going on to establish their RAW EDGES DESIGN STUDIO later that year. While Yael's interests include turning two-dimensional sheet materials into curvaceous functional forms, Shay is fascinated by how things move, function, and react. Their collection of seven living islands was created with surface specialist Caesarstone, while Stack, their innovative chest of drawers made in collaboration with Established & Sons, is part of the permanent collection at MoMA in New York. Together they have worked with such luminaries as Cappellini, Kvadrat, and Stella McCartney while receiving several highly respected awards such as the **Wallpaper** Design Award, the Elle Deco International Design Award for Best Furniture, and Designer of the Future from Design Miami/Basel. •

Commerce and the Collective

Craftsmen have long congregated in guilds, unions, and organizations for both business support and a sense of community. The practical benefits of working together are self-evident—the possibility to become stronger trade partners, collaborate on marketing endeavors, share knowledge, and reinforce their stability as small or growing businesses. From the Art Worker's Guild founded on the principles set out by William Morris to the Wiener Werkstätte at the turn of the century, differing but complementary crafts have always benefited from coexisting in a collective environment. Collaborative showcases throughout history, such as the world's fairs of the last century, were of great significance to the craftspeople of the time, and this still rings true today as crafted products compete in an increasingly competitive global trade landscape. Enthusiastic entrepreneurs have presented crafted products in a new light at their point of sale, be it with luxury positioning in a retail environment, the rarefied confines of a gallery or introducing them to e-commerce. In doing this, crafted products can benefit from greater diversification and a wider reach, in order to further establish their place in the broader cultural environment.

Since 2012, THE NEW CRAFTSMEN initiative has worked with a selection of Britain's finest makers to showcase the materials, skills, and craft products of the British Isles. Founded in London, The New Craftsmen currently represents a network of over 75 artisans and makers working in textiles, silverware, furniture, ceramics, jewelry, glassware, and beyond. Showcasing and selling a selected range of products, limited editions, and exclusive collaborations in their Mayfair store and online, they present and display objects that are deeply connected to culture and place.

Forging networks between makers and clients, they offer their customers, interior designers, and architects a range of services that enable them to customize, commission, and collaborate with the craftsmen on bespoke pieces. Envisioning a future of sustainable luxury through dedication to makers, materials, methods, and designs, they represent amongst others Doe Leather, a Black Country leather goods workshop that works with hand-waxed hides, Edmond Byrne, an internationally acclaimed Irish glass blower, and Grant McCaig, a Scottish silver, gold, and metal smith who is exhibited internationally.

Founded in 2000 by Rachel Wythe-Moran and Simon Watkins in East London's market district, LABOUR AND WAIT is a retail space offering hardware, garden tools, and clothing that adhere to their ethos of functional design, which promotes classics to keep and love. Due to the founders' frustration in having to design and redesign products and ranges every season, not allowing for products to mature and establish themselves, they decided to set up shop with

simple, timeless, honestly designed products where quality and utility are intrinsic. Gradually sourcing the products that fitted their ethos, they are now established as a leading voice in the independent shopping landscape, with concessions in Dover Street Market in London and several in Japan through Bshop. •

Innovation

Couillaud, Babette Fischer, and Claudia Rannow, they have exhibited in Inter-Connected during New York Design Week, Destination:Portugal at the MoMA, and the ten-year anniversary of the Guggenheim, Berlin.

Innovation is at the heart of craftmaking as it is at the heart of its practitioners—while assembly line production methods make a run of perfectly similar and equal objects, a craftsperson works one-on-one with an object, requiring his or her full attention. This constant assessment of the process results in a stream of new ideas, with the craftsperson constantly reassessing the best way to execute the work. Although today handcrafted techniques and handmade materials are often considered a luxury, it's easy to forget that many crafts were once a question of necessity rather than choice. With the advent of technologically advanced production methods, cheap construction materials, and outsourced, unskilled labor, it may seem anachronistic to think of craft as innovative. But it always has been, and in many ways it still is. Within craft guilds and trainee programs, the apprenticeship system means that young students often spend years learning under a master craftsman before being allowed to take on clients themselves. This underlines the importance not only of keeping certain crafts and traditions alive, but also of passing the necessary skills onto the next generation. Today this spirit of transferred knowledge is kept alive by many brands, which collaborate with design schools and other initiatives to engender the same culture of skill sharing from a young age.

Founded in 2005, **THE HOME PROJECT** is a design studio founded by Álbio Nascimento and Kathi Stertzig in Berlin that focuses on responsible design innovation and a spirit of exploration between people and place. It's an integrated design practice dedicated to cultural research as an approach to work, with an authentic, engaged, and sustainable material culture in order to serve and provide an alternative way for clients and partners to obtain crafted elements for their interior and architectural projects. Using design as a communication tool, they curate and collaborate exhibitions and showcases for craftsmen they find, and connect them to buyers and their e-commerce network. Representing such makers as Anne

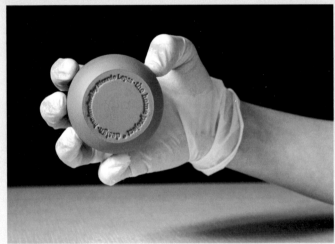

The
MAKERS

BÖLE TANNERY
LEATHERWORKERS

LOCATED JUST SOUTH OF THE ARCTIC CIRCLE IN THE REMOTE SWEDISH TOWN OF BÖLE, THIS FOURTH-GENERATION SPRUCE BARK LEATHER TANNERY IS THE LAST OF ITS KIND IN THE WORLD.

Böle Tannery is one of the last standing bark tanneries in the world and a purveyor to the Swedish royal court. Founded in 1899, they craft each leather product with considerable passion and dedication, combining beauty, functionality, and durability. With a guarantee of fifteen years on their products, Böle are particularly famous for their rucksacks and briefcases, and their commitment to sustainable practices using spruce bark and vegetable tanning.

All products are crafted under the same roof in the small village of Böle just south of the Arctic Circle in Sweden. Tanning, the transformation of raw hides into leather, can be achieved in various ways, but the slow process of spruce bark tanning provides the leather with a unique color and an undamaged surface that are so highly valued, no further treatment or dye is necessary. The process also makes the leather stiff and durable, which is useful for certain Böle products. It is made by mixing water from the Pite River with spruce bark flakes in open vats into which Swedish cattle hides are placed. To tan a single hide can take up to a year, and Anders Sandlund, the fourth generation proprietor of Böle Tannery explains, "We think it's worth it when we see the end result: a beautiful leather, naturally colored by spruce bark. It is unlike anything else."

Böle is primarily known for its rucksacks and briefcases. The rucksacks are made from Nordic reindeer skin, the finest and thickest available, which is tanned using organic products. The hides are vegetable tanned into smooth yet strong leather with Böle Tannery honoring a rather scaled-back, simple style: the only hint of decoration on the rucksacks is the plate of reindeer horn, a "plate that has been crafted and engraved with the owner's initials by a true master, in accordance with old Sami traditions." Böle briefcases, the tannery's specialty, reach a level of perfection that can only be achieved through the highest levels of traditional craftsmanship. They are made from a single hide of Swedish cattle and are tanned in a mix of spruce bark and Pite river water for nine to twelve months. The briefcases are numbered and come with a free annual service for fifteen years after the date of purchase. Sandlund asserts, "Our products are made to last and to age with style."

Sustainability is also of considerable concern to Böle tanners. Their immediate goal is to be the most sustainable company in the leather industry. Sandlund comments, "The ultimate goal, however, is no less than to become a globally recognized benchmark for sustainable business." •

The Double Minister briefcase is one of Böle Tannery's signature products.

BÖLE BRIEFCASES, THE
TANNERY'S SPECIALTY, REACH
A LEVEL OF PERFECTION
THAT CAN ONLY BE ACHIEVED
THROUGH THE HIGHEST
LEVELS OF TRADITIONAL
CRAFTSMANSHIP.

left: Master leathercraft tools.

above: Jan Sandlund and his son,
Anders, run the tannery.

THE ULTIMATE GOAL,
HOWEVER, IS NO LESS THAN
TO BECOME A GLOBALLY
RECOGNIZED BENCHMARK FOR
SUSTAINABLE BUSINESS.

The Böle flagship store
in Piteå, Sweden.

right: Servicing a briefcase in the
Böle workshop. Master tanner
Jan Sandlund moves hides in the
tanning vat.

FRANK LEDER
FASHION DESIGNER

INSPIRED BY THE TAILORING AND HERITAGE OF TRADITIONAL GERMAN WORKWEAR, FRANK LEDER HAS TURNED HIS HAND TO CLOTHING COLLECTIONS AND A RANGE OF NATURAL BODYCARE PRODUCTS THAT EMPLOY HAND-COLLECTED ORGANIC BOTANICALS.

From the first stages of conception to the finishing touches of production, Frank Leder's eponymous fashion collections are as German as can be. The graduate of Central Saint Martins College of Art and Design pays homage to his roots by fashioning clothing lines inspired by German workwear and tailoring, reflecting Bavarian sensibilities, including a penchant for the practical, close attention to detail, and flawless quality—but always with a touch of whimsy. Founded in 2000, he started out by designing womenswear but has since transitioned his focus to his eponymous men's label. Now based in Berlin, his appreciation for his cultural heritage shines through all of his creative endeavors, whether fashion, grooming products, or even furniture design.

Growing up in Nuremberg, the outdoors were an important part of Leder's upbringing, and he fondly recalls spending time foraging for mushrooms and going fishing with his father. Romantic memories of his childhood are apparent in Leder's entire brand aesthetic, which conjures up images of simpler times. The past, and German history more specifically, is an overarching theme in the clothing. Tailored cuts recall the typical clothes worn by German workmen, such as miners, bakers, and butchers, during colonial times. A deep appreciation for nature extends to a partiality for the natural—Leder avoids synthetic materials. The clothes are made from the finest traditional German fabrics such as Deutschleder and Shladminger but also include high-quality wool, linen, and cotton, and most buttons are original antique pieces from the 1920s and 30s. Yet, while the garments may be inspired by the past, they are far from old-fashioned. Their retro flair is paired with innovative contemporary cuts that are easy to wear and always interesting to look at. The touch of whimsy and subtle humor that Leder adds to his work play an important role in making the clothes essentially modern: for one of his

Designer Frank Leder in his studio, surrounded by sewing patterns.

collections, Leder dyed fabric with strong German beer and sold the pieces with antique beer mugs from the 1930s. From the design process down to packaging, Frank Leder is not afraid to experiment and continually pushes the boundaries of novelty, all the while remaining faithful to his vision.

Leder's vision also extends to a line of refined

FROM THE DESIGN PROCESS DOWN TO PACKAGING, FRANK LEDER IS NOT AFRAID TO EXPERIMENT AND CONTINUALLY PUSHES THE BOUNDARIES OF NOVELTY, ALL THE WHILE REMAINING FAITHFUL TO HIS VISION.

above: "Holz," Frank Leder's Fall/Winter 2010 collection, features masculine clothes that are both practical and fashionable.

bodycare products that he calls Tradition, produced in limited quantities from carefully selected plants and herbs. Tradition is another testament to the designer's standards of quality. The organic ingredients,

hand-collected for each product, are selected, harvested, and extracted with the greatest care and consideration for the environment. As implied by the name, the bodycare line is a consistent extension of Frank Leder clothing collections as it celebrates and shows respect for the past, and indeed, the recipes used for Tradition products have been passed down through several generations. The collection includes products such as the Bavarian Hand Soap, Honey Hand Lotion, Elderflower Body Wash, and Wheat Beer Shampoo. Every last detail of the packaging is also carefully thought-through with products presented in glass bottles with vintage Bakelite screw caps, inside beautifully illustrated paper boxes.

Frank Leder prefers to avoid commercial trends, choosing instead to inhabit a realm of his own where he is more interested in creating highly personal collections than appealing to the masses—an attitude that has won him a select and loyal following. ●

above: Limited edition German oak
bath oil manufactured with traditional
artisan methods in Austria.

left: Frank Leder's designs are
inspired by the history of ordinary
working-class German men.

ALDO BAKKER
EXPERIMENTAL STUDIO

WORKING WITH A WIDE RANGE OF MATERIALS

AND INSPIRED BY THE ESSENTIAL

GEOMETRY OF CÉZANNE AND BRANCUSI,

ACCLAIMED INDUSTRIAL DESIGNER

ALDO BAKKER FINDS CRAFTED PROCESSES

INTEGRAL TO HIS WORK.

Aldo Bakker, born in 1971 to acclaimed avant-garde jewelry artist Emmy van Leersum, and Gijs Bakker, co-founder of the influential conceptual design collective Droog, is a Dutch designer of furniture and small household products. His work traverses the notions of art, ritual, and function, and is often shaped around the clean, soft forms, which give themselves naturally and optimize the functionality of an object. Working from his own studio in a 1930s brick house in Amsterdam since 1994, his practice employs a "form-follows-function" ethos, developing products that are refined, minimal, and elegant, and crafted in natural colors. His pieces can be found in several permanent collections including those at the Victoria & Albert Museum in London, the Stedelijk Museum in Amsterdam, and the Museum Boijmans Van Beuningen in Rotterdam.

Without a formal design education, Bakker is a craftsman who challenges the perception of time and timelessness rather than focusing on fashion or zeitgeist. He rarely approaches his designs with the desire to solve a problem but prefers instead to focus on the purity of form by studying and sketching. This allows him to establish whether the form he is looking at in any given moment can be translated into an object, and what that object or image might be. He is deeply inspired by the approach of artists like Cézanne or Brancusi, who attempted to distill a mountain or a plate of apples down to its geometric essence, often leading to new interpretations of how the object can actually be used and its ultimate function. Aldo comments, "My designs demand slowness and awareness, time and attention. The enormous investment of attention and care that brings my products to life only becomes visible after a considerable amount of time. The precision of form and materials will eventually lead to new uses and experiences of the content. I question the most common significance of products and thus also their use. In an ideal situation, every object takes on its own character and gains its own legitimacy. My designs are not based on fashion. They are unique pieces, not necessarily understandable at a glance, but meant for a slow, layer-by-layer exploration."

Designer Aldo Bakker
(left) in his workshop.

"MY DESIGNS DEMAND SLOWNESS AND AWARENESS, TIME AND ATTENTION. THE ENORMOUS INVESTMENT OF ATTENTION AND CARE THAT BRINGS MY PRODUCTS TO LIFE ONLY BECOMES VISIBLE AFTER A CONSIDERABLE AMOUNT OF TIME."

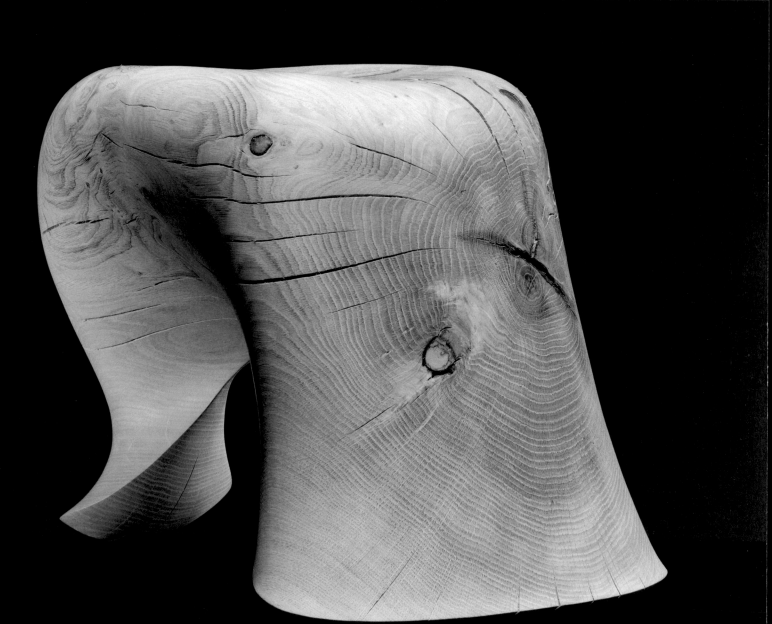

left: Tonus is a piece from the Wood
Collection. It was handmade
using a single solid block of wood.

above: Silver salt cellars made in
collaboration with master craftsman
Jan Matthesius.

His galvanized copper watering can, part of the Copper Collection, unites the spout, container, and handle in one continuous form with no distinction or line between the three parts, which are melded together. The size of the tube is the same as standard copper water tubes, but with a slight dent at its end so the water will flow back down into the vessel after pouring. Combining traditional and modern techniques, Bakker uses molding, galvanizing, and lacquering which result in a wide range of products including stools, soy pourers, candleholders, bowls, and saucepans. His Urishi three-legged stoo—comprised of just three pieces of wood with a round convex top, a spindle-shaped front leg, and a block shaped like half an apple that forms the stubby back legs—evolved over time from shapes he had previously visited in his

designs. Working with skilled Dutch and European artisans to finish his pieces, he has been able to perfect his craft in silver, glass, and ceramic alongside his favorite material wood.

Adding another level of intrigue to his objects, Bakker entices the user to think twice before pouring, drinking, sitting down in a chair, or sprinkling salt or pepper onto a dish. By questioning the monotony of such tasks and making the user perform all these casual and daily ritual acts with renewed attention and concentration, Bakker's designs and their capricious nature invite the user to grasp the unexpected and take stock of the routine of our daily customs. •

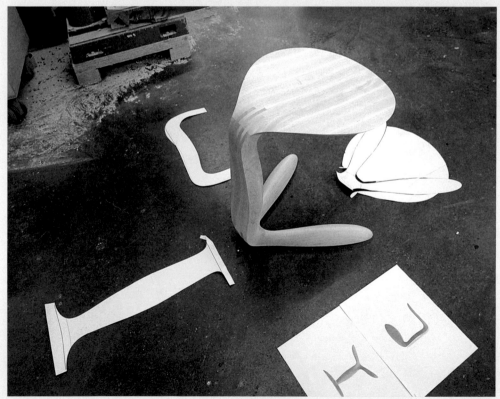

The sculptural stool Anura has been hand-carved from one solid piece of maple wood by long-time collaborator and master woodcrafter Rutger Graas.

top right: The Milk Can is part of a series of fluid porcelain tableware pieces.

ASAHIYAKI
POTTERY WORKSHOP

HAILING FROM THE TOWN OF UJI, KYOTO, THE TRADITIONAL CENTER OF TEA CULTIVATION IN JAPAN, THE ASAHIYAKI WORKSHOP HAS BEEN RUNNING CONTINUOUSLY FOR OVER 400 YEARS THROUGH 15 GENERATIONS OF THE MATSUBAYASHI FAMILY, CRAFTING DELICATE POTTERY FOR THE ANCIENT ART OF TEA PREPARATION.

A sahiyaki is a pottery and porcelain workshop based in Uji, Japan, whose products celebrate the subtle intricacies of the Japanese tea ceremony. Tea drinking in Japan has a long and venerable history, and its ceremonial preparation was originally influenced by Zen Buddhist practices. The Asahiyaki pottery has been in continuous production for over four hundred years, creating tea bowls for serving "whipped tea" to the nobility, warrior rulers, and tea masters. The range includes teaware uniquely designed to preserve the subtle flavors of Japanese tea, with the delicate pieces being handcrafted by members of the Matsubayashi family, who have passed down their accumulated skill and expertise for fifteen generations. Bowls, vases, trays, teapots, and teacups are carefully produced in a striking range of glazed hues including blood red, mint and forest greens, powder pink, and sky and ocean blues. The style became known as one of the Seven Famous Kilns of

Enshu, following the preferences of the tea ceremony master Kobori Enshu (1579–1647).

Introduced to Japan in the 12th century by the priest Eisai, tea quickly became closely associated with Japanese life and a unique culture formed around its preparation and enjoyment. Uji developed as the representative tea-producing region under the patronage of the shogunate, and the Asahiyaki pottery was among one of the first workshops in Japan to begin marking its wares with a seal. Each generation of the Matsubayashi family has used a personalized seal to distinguish their work, and also to mark different phases of their careers. Along with the Raku workshop in Kyoto, the Matsubayashi family is one of just two ceramic lineages to have received its seal from the imperial family of Japan.

Asahiyaki pottery is made from clay that is sourced from within the region, and creates the gently expressive mottled patterns that are typical of their

Decorative details are added to a vase using a knife in the pottery workshop.

ASAHIYAKI POTTERY IS MADE
FROM CLAY THAT IS SOURCED
FROM WITHIN THE REGION,
WHICH GIVES RISE TO THE
GENTLY EXPRESSIVE MOTTLED
PATTERNS THAT ARE TYPICAL
OF THEIR PRODUCTS.

right: Tea bowls, cups, and trays
are handcrafted using potter's wheels,
lopes, and gifted hands.

top: Inside the kiln.

products. "The production of Asahiyaki begins by digging the clay ourselves from the mountain in Uji," says Yusuke. "The clay is dried and sifted to remove the dross, and mixed with water, and then squeezed to the right firmness for making pottery." The raw and organic elegance of the vessel forms are created by the technique of throwing on the potter's wheel through attention to detail in the shaping of the rim or the angle of the facet cutting. The current general master, Asahiyaki XV Matsubayashi Hosai, blends the traditions of the workshop with his own modern aesthetic sense, often intertwined with his son Yusuke's youthful spin, in order to maximize the experience and taste of each unique tea. "Asahiyaki has very high skills cultivated by traditions in the *mizubiki* [shaping] and shaving processes," he adds.

After shaping, the pottery is dried for two to five days, and fired for the first time. Initially it's fired for five hours at 800°C and then a glaze is applied. The glaze is an important factor in determining the color of the finished pieces, and obtaining the signature translucent tonalities for which Asahiyaki is known. After glazing, the pieces are fired again at 1200°C to 1300°C. "The difficulty of pottery is in the firing," concludes Yusuke. "Although the pottery's color depends on the selection of clay, the glaze mixture, and how you apply the glaze, if the final firing does not go well, everything is ruined. With Asahiyaki, we fire the kiln while daily improving the skills that we have accumulated." •

PATRIK MUFF
JEWELRY DESIGNER

A STORY OF CONTRADICTIONS, PATRIK MUFF'S

REBELLIOUS EXTERIOR BELIES THE DELICATE SENSITIVITY

OF HIS JEWELRY CREATIONS.

Born into a family of craftsmen in 1962, Swiss jewelry designer Patrik Muff trained as a gold-smith and since 1998 has lived and worked in Munich, Germany. The heavily tattooed artist brings a certain edge to the design of his pieces that evoke an eclectic mix of religious, mythical, and dark fairytale-like imagery. Muff is uncompromising when it comes to quality, with only the finest materials used in his creations, including gemstones, pearls, and noble metals such as silver and gold.

Muff was born in Switzerland and studied art in Cologne, New York, and London before moving to Munich where he is based today. His collections are highly sought after, yet increasing demand has not changed the meticulous process that Muff employs on each piece of jewelry he produces, nor has it widened the scope of the brand's distribution, which remains exclusive to Germany. Since the inception of his practice in 1991, Muff has collaborated with an impressive range of fashion houses and artists such as Birkenstock, Puma, and Jenny Holzer. For Birkenstock, he created a collection of sandals in crocodile embossed calfskin with 18-carat gold buckles with tiger eye gemstones. The most notable partnership remains one that took place in 2008 with renowned porcelain house Nymphenburg for which Muff designed an 18-piece, handmade collection, featuring hearts, lilies, crosses, anchors, and bones, called Essentials. Muff spent time researching

Nymphenburg's archives that date back to the eighteenth century to develop a collection of jewelry that represents what he considers the essentials of human existence: faith, love, hope, and death. Inspired by Franz Ignaz Günther's skull dating back to 1756, the collection paired gold, silver, rubies, and diamonds with Nymphenburg white porcelain made from clay that was aged for two years in a cellar before it could be molded. Striking jewelry pieces in the shapes of strong sacred symbols are the result of the successful collaboration.

FAITH AND DEATH ARE A CONSISTENT MOTIF IN PATRIK MUFF'S COLLECTIONS.

Faith and death are a consistent motif in Patrik Muff's collections. Skulls with baroque ornamentation, angel wings, and elaborate crosses appear in many of the designer's collections—always with the rebellious touch of rock'n'roll for which Muff is now renowned. Nature also plays an important role in his creations, which conjure images of flora and fauna, and which often feature embellished insects such as spiders, beetles, and bees. Similarly to a tattoo, Patrik Muff conceives of a piece of jewelry as an extension of the person wearing it; it is a mark of individuality that provides insight into their personal history. •

Swiss jewelry designer Patrik Muff in his Munich atelier.

PATRIK MUFF CONCEIVES OF A
PIECE OF JEWELRY AS AN EXTEN-
SION OF THE PERSON WEARING
IT; IT IS A MARK OF INDIVIDU-
ALITY THAT PROVIDES INSIGHT
INTO THEIR PERSONAL HISTORY.

left: Pieces from various collections
inspired by religion, mythical
creatures, and fairytales.

Tradition meets eccentricity: in
2014 Patrik Muff collaborated with
Ketel One Vodka and redesigned
the copper kettle.

KLAR SEIFEN
SOAP MANUFACTURE

**BASED IN HEIDELBERG, GERMANY'S OLDEST
SOAP MAKER USES ONLY NATURAL OILS AND VEGETABLE
PRODUCTS THAT HAVE BEEN CULTIVATED
USING ORGANIC PRACTICES.**

Klar Seifen, Germany's oldest soap manufacturer based in Heidelberg, was founded by Philipp Klar in 1840 and has since been passed down through five generations. For over 170 years they have used only the highest quality ingredients to produce some of the world's finest soaps. Ecological responsibility is an important part of the Klar Seifen ethos, with a concerted effort to minimize the company's impact on the environment as much as possible, while craftsmanship remains the backbone of the business.

The first step in manufacturing Klar Seifen soaps consists in making the soap base. This process has essentially remained the same since the first recipes for soap, dating back to the Sumerians 5,000 years ago. Oils and fats are first of all boiled with an alkali, usually sodium or potassium hydroxide. While many industrial soap manufacturers use animal fats and artificial preservatives in their production processes, Klar Seifen use only vegetable oils that have been organically cultivated. When the soap base is finished, it is mixed with other carefully selected ingredients, such as jojoba oil, grape seed extract, or flower petals. High-quality perfume or pure essential oils such as lavender or rosemary oil are also added to the soap base concoction at this point. The soap

base is then rolled and pelleted, a five-step process by which a homogeneous soap mass is formed. The fourth step consists of passing the soap mass under a special press, which heats and molds the mass into a cuboid strand. It is then cut into equal parts and pressed into shape, with some of the presses and molds being over a century old. The final step is the packaging, which is done with as much care and attention to detail as all the previous steps: Each bar of soap is inspected before it is wrapped and packaged and ready to leave the factory.

Klar Seifen continually consults with dermatologists to marry old savoir-faire with the new demands of modern life, thereby developing products that are mild to even the most sensitive skins. Mixing the old with the new is a company-wide method, as recipes that date back over a hundred years are combined with innovative ingredients to spruce up time-tested classics such as the Klar Seifen peony, linden flower, or lily of the valley soaps. Niels Klar, the latest Klar family member at the head of the business, is in charge of ensuring that the standards of quality and authenticity continue to be met as the brand expands to include a new range of products as it looks to the future. •

Klar Seifen owner Niels Klar took over the business from his two uncles.

MIXING THE OLD WITH THE NEW IS A COMPANY-WIDE METHOD, AS RECIPES THAT DATE BACK OVER A HUNDRED YEARS ARE COMBINED WITH INNOVATIVE INGREDIENTS.

left: The soap mass is pressed with
a traditional mold.

above: A pelleting machine
processes a variety of ingredients into
a homogeneous soap mass.

ORGELBAU KLAIS
PIPE ORGAN BUILDER

A MUCH-RESPECTED NAME IN THE DESIGN, RESTORATION, AND MANUFACTURE OF PIPE ORGANS, ORGELBAU KLAIS HAS CREATED UNIQUE PIECES FOR CHURCHES AND CONCERT HALLS THAT CAN BE FOUND ON EVERY CONTINENT AROUND THE WORLD.

Orgelbau Klais has been designing, manufacturing, and restoring pipe organs in Bonn since 1882. Johannes Klais Sr., the founder of the business that is still run by the family to this day, was considered to be an innovative genius in his day, as he was the first to build an electronically controlled pipe organ as early as 1906. Klais' vision and passion for the instrument have been passed down from generation to generation and, today, Philipp Klais is at the head of the workshop, ensuring that his great-grandfather's values continue to be honored.

In order to make the highest-quality organs, Orgelbau Klais is divided into six departments, each led by a specialist in their own specific craft. The departments reflect all the necessary steps required to produce a Klais pipe organ, from the initial selection and cutting of the wood to the pre-voicing of the organ. Mostly fine-grained spruce and long-seasoned oak woods are used but the workshop is fully equipped to work with metal, wood, and even leather used for sealing purposes. As soon as a specified level of progress has been made on each commission, pre-installation takes place within the workshop's great hall. Casework and internal structures are assembled, wind ducts built to measure, action parts installed, and the biggest pipes put into place. The full technical installation happens directly in the organ's new home.

During the second generation of the workshop's existence, the founder's son, Hans Klais, was the first to incorporate modern ergonomic principles to the inner workings of an organ. He then had the privilege of building pipe organs for the world's fair in Brussels in 1935 and for the Bruges and Ghent cathedrals in 1936—a testament to Orgelbau Klais' craftsmanship. Following the Second World War and the workshop's reconstruction, Hans Klais and his team also built Cologne Cathedral's organ directly in the nave. The geographical scope of Orgelbau Klais organs dramatically expanded as soon as better modes of transportation and shipping were developed, and today Klais instruments can be found all over the world, including in the Esplanade Concert Hall in Singapore, in Saint Peter's Lutheran Church in New York City, and in the Queensland Performing Arts Center in Brisbane, Australia.

Throughout the decades, the Klais family members have pursued their passion for the imposing pipe organ both with forward-thinking vision and time-tested traditional techniques. The dedicated craftsmen behind Orgelbau Klais strive to revive what they esteem to be "the transcendent aura of the organ." •

In 2007, Orgelbau Klais replaced all the pipes in the Catedral del Pilar in Zaragoza, Spain within the original organ body dating back to 1590.

left: Inside the Catedral
del Pilar's pipe organ.

right: The pipe manufactory
in Bonn, Germany.

THE KLAIS FAMILY MEMBERS
HAVE PURSUED THEIR PASSION
FOR THE IMPOSING PIPE ORGAN
BOTH WITH FORWARD-THINKING
VISION AND TIME-TESTED
TRADITIONAL TECHNIQUES.

left: The organ at St. Elisabeth's church in Marburg, Germany, made by Orgelbau Klais.

above: Philipp Klais, owner of Orgelbau Klais.

right: A craftsman thins out a sheet of iron.

JAN KATH
CARPET DESIGNER

DESIGNER JAN K ATH BRINGS THE ANCIENT CRAFT OF CARPET WEAVING UP TO DATE WITH STRIKING CONTEMPORARY DESIGNS THAT PLAY ON TRADITIONAL MOTIFS, AS WELL AS AN EMPHASIS ON SUSTAINABILITY AND FAIR-TRADE PRACTICES.

A s a mainstay of Oriental craftsmanship for many centuries, embroidered carpets were intended not only for floors, but hung on walls as works of art. This is a custom that Bochum-based Jan Kath, the founder of Jan Kath Design, is looking to reinstate in his work. Considering himself a "couturier for floors," his daring designs, which incorporate shocking colors, unsettling patterns, and mirage-like pixel veiling, have once again elevated the carpet from the floors onto the walls.

While his designs are conceived in his creative department with his design colleague Dino Feldmann, in the Ruhr region of Germany, his carpets are realized and handwoven in Kathmandu, Nepal or in Azilal in Morocco's Atlas Mountains. Worldwide, more than 2,500 artisanal carpet weavers work for his company relying on centuries old weaving traditions and manufacturing processes, many of which are still carried out by family-run workshops. While the hand production is rigorous and time-consuming, Jan Kath Design has created a business model where the majority of the orders are specific to the individual customer with regards to size, format, color, and materials. This, combined with a streamlined global distribution network, has allowed flexibility, customization, and collaboration to become focus points of the company's ethos, which in turn has led to custom-design projects for such behemoths of the interiors world as Christian Liaigre, Matteo Thun, and Peter Marino.

Jan Kath has no formal design training but his instinctive eye for intricate motifs belies the complex processes behind his work. His hand-knotted collections are made in Nepal from the finest and most robust materials. Tibetan highland wool is spun by hand after having being brought down by shepherded yaks from the mountains and washed in the rivers. Only ecologically tested dyes from Switzerland are used and in addition to the wool, the finest Chinese silks and yarns from stinging-nettle fiber help create lustrous reflections in the finished carpet. These unique, naturally processed materials together with the manual weaving techniques, which have hardly changed for hundreds of years, give each carpet its unique character. "I adore these different forms of expression, and I have made it my mission to keep them alive," explains Jan. "In Morocco, for example, we have adopted a technique used by the nomadic Berbers that results in a rustic, archaic effect. This seemingly unsophisticated method causes the yarn to open on the surface, which is the only way to allow the rich sheen of the white wool from the Atlas highlands to come into its own." Referring to the Turkish knotting method, he adds, "We use this technique for projects in Anatolia and Agra, in the ancient Mughal capitals of India and in our experimental workshop in Afghanistan. After the carpet has grown inch by inch over several months on the loom and the last knot has been tied, the second stage can begin: washing. This

Carpet designer Jan Kath
in front of one of his masterpieces.

above: All of Jan Kath's carpets are
hand-woven in Kathmandu, Nepal or
in Azilal in Morocco's Atlas mountains
using each location's respective
traditional techniques passed on from
generation to generation.

right: A photorealistic carpet from
the "Spacecrafted" series.

WORLDWIDE MORE THAN
2,500 ARTISANAL CARPET WEAVERS
WORK FOR HIS COMPANY
RELYING ON CENTURIES-OLD
WEAVING TRADITIONS AND MANU-
FACTURING PROCESSES, MANY OF
WHICH ARE STILL CARRIED OUT
BY FAMILY-RUN WORKSHOPS.

left: The "Erased Heritage" collection pays homage to the traditional Oriental carpet.

is an important process that has a major influence on the final look of a piece. It can bring out the brilliance of the colors or give them an emphatically subdued appearance. The wash is therefore responsible for deciding whether a carpet looks brand new or centuries old. In order to give pieces their final shape, they are stretched on a frame when still wet and carefully laid out to dry in the sun in inner courtyards and on the roofs of houses."

In addition to his handwoven carpets, Jan Kath also offers manually tufted carpets, which differ from their handwoven counterparts in that the individual threads are not individually tied around a warp thread, but instead shot from a tufting gun onto a prepared base material. This shortens the production time considerably and makes it possible to create much larger carpets. These carpets express different characteristics with their combination of velour and winding textures, varied pile heights, and diverse use of materials such as silk, wool, rayon, and hemp. This was the method chosen by Prince Albert II for the 103-meter-long red carpet that lined the aisle of the church where he married Charlene Whitstock, as the whole piece had to be finished in just two months. Jan Kath's carpets succeed in bridging an ancient craft, with a contemporary approach and striking, elegant aesthetic. The opportunity for high levels of customization coupled with his dedication to fair wage practices, close monitoring of working conditions, and ecological sustainability suggest a company that is well prepared for the challenges of the future. •

NAKAGAWA MOKKOUGEI WOODWORKERS

SPECIALIZING IN TRADITIONAL KI-OKE HANDCRAFTED WOODEN BUCKETS, THREE GENERATIONS OF THE MOKKOUGEI FAMILY HAVE EACH BROUGHT SOMETHING NEW TO THIS ANCIENT AND VENERABLE ART FORM.

Founded in 1961, Nakagawa Mokkougei is a third-generation master woodworking firm from Kyoto that specializes in traditional Japanese wooden vessels. The grandfather of the family, Kameichi, began his apprenticeship with Tarugen, a long-established bucket-making workshop, when he was only nine years old, and spent forty years there perfecting the craft, before setting out on his own under the Nakagawa Mokkougei name. Today the company keeps two studios, one in Kyoto run by Kameichi's son, Kiyotsugu Nakagawa, and one in Shiga, run by his grandson Shuji Nakagawa, who is also a contemporary artist. The family have received several awards and accolades for their continued championing of traditional Japanese craftsmanship and Kiyotsugu is considered something of a national treasure in the country, having passed on his expertise through years of dedication to his son Shuji. Renowned for crafting traditional buckets, known as *ki-oke,* Nakagawa

Mokkougei makes use of techniques that have remained largely unchanged since they were developed 700 years ago during the Muromanchi era. At one time, a typical Japanese family would have had several buckets like this in each household, for uses such as storing rice or miso, but today they are used as contemporary applications as champagne buckets, stools, tables, and even bathtubs. Making use of Japanese cypress, cedar, and umbrella pine woods, each have their own unique colors and properties, as well as high tolerances to water, meaning the vessels and other items are ideal for use with liquids.

There are more than ten processes involved in creating one of Nagakawa Mokkougei's pieces. Firstly, the wood has to be dried, which can take a few months for wooden chips, or up to several years for full logs. The logs are then sliced into rounds and chopped into workable strips using a machete. The pieces are then delicately refined with planes of

Shuji Nakagawa is the third generation of traditional woodworkers in his family.

left: The Indigo Gradient Table is the second object in a series of pieces to follow the success of the Ki-oke stool designed by Danish design studio OeO.

above: The Ki-oke stool fuses fine Kyoto woodcrafting with Western sensibilities.

varying thicknesses to achieve the smooth, seamless surface seen on the finished products. The pieces are whittled on the surface to adjust the gradient and angle, before being joined with bamboo nails; a metal hoop placed around the circumference holds everything in place. Once the pieces are assembled, the vessel is then whittled again, on both the inside and outside, before the metal hoop is tightened for a final time, the base is attached, and the completed piece is polished to perfection. Today, Shuji has advanced this traditional practice with the use of complex technical drawings to allow him to create shapes and forms that would have previously not been possible, including triangular and teardrop-shaped buckets. Obviously, to create a watertight vessel, the constituent elements have to be cut and shaped to minute tolerances, and this becomes all the more

RENOWNED FOR CRAFTING TRADITIONAL BUCKETS, NAKAGAWA MOKKOUGEI MAKE USE OF TECHNIQUES THAT HAVE REMAINED LARGELY UNCHANGED SINCE THEY WERE DEVELOPED 700 YEARS AGO.

remarkable when you consider that every part of the process is executed entirely by hand. Nakagawa Mokkougei has recently collaborated with Danish design studio OeO on the Ki-oke Stool, as well as being part of the Japan Handmade initiative, which celebrates the traditional crafts of the Kyoto region, bringing them to an international market and aiming to "introduce the world to the tactile pleasure, poetry, and soul of Japanese design." •

GOLEM
TILE AND CERAMIC WORKSHOP

COLLABORATING WITH LEADING ARCHITECTS AND RESTORERS AROUND THE WORLD, GOLEM ARCHITECTURAL CERAMICS PRODUCE A HUGE RANGE OF HANDCRAFTED TILES AND CERAMIC ARCHITECTURAL DETAILS THAT BRING FADED BUILDINGS SENSITIVELY BACK TO LIFE.

Founder of Golem, Tomas Grzimek, established his business after East and West Germany were reunited in 1990.

Golem Kunst und Baukeramik (Arts and Architectural Ceramics) specializes in custom ceramics for the restoration of culturally valuable buildings, and since 2002 has also produced a wide range of hand-painted art nouveau tiles based on classic historical motifs. Founded by Tomas Grzimek, the company has a strong history of collaborating with leading architects and architectural restorers from all over Europe, focusing on the restoration of buildings from all eras. "The foundation of the manufactory happened in reaction to the massive changes in East Germany during German reunification in 1990," says Tomas. "Until that point, ceramicists had been needed, since everything was in short supply, especially original and unusual products. Everything ceramicists produced, from pots to figures, was thankfully bought by state-owned galleries and shops. There were many collectors of ceramics and people were constantly in search of interesting gifts. After the fall of the Berlin Wall, it was not deficiency but an oversupply of beautiful things from all over the world that prevailed. If you

wanted to continue as a ceramicist you had to learn a second profession, you had to learn to promote your products and yourself. Extending our range to the reproduction of historical tiles helped us gain more independence. I recaptured the feeling of producing something that is needed."

In the former barn of a manor house near Berlin, Tomas and his team create a vast range of architectural ceramics, from hand-molded bricks to terracotta sculptures, and painted borders, as well as contemporary architectural details rendered in ceramic. Among the oldest known construction materials, clay and ceramics are astounding in their versatility of application. Particularly impressive are the terracotta craftspeople, who require a high degree of sculptural proficiency to create the original models that are used for casting a mold and producing duplicates. While the small batch runs will produce a consistent result, there is still the sense that every piece has its own minute but distinctly individual characteristics. A staggering 80 percent of the work in the Golem

A volute made of architectural ceramic for Schwerin Castle in Germany.

studio is still done by hand, simply because there is no other alternative. This is especially relevant when dealing with ceramics for historical restoration work, which constitutes a significant proportion of Golem's business. If the replacement pieces were made with a machine, they wouldn't have the same look or feel as the pieces they are replacing, which were perhaps first installed 200 years ago. The company has been responsible for contributing restoration components to several notable projects, including the Kommandantenhaus in Berlin and the world famous Harrods department store in London.

Each new commission for Golem provides its own challenges, with orders ranging from the domestic to the monumental. For example, certain plaster molds for making tiles can only be used to cast around 40 tiles before they have to be replaced, otherwise the edges of the tiles start to lose their definition and sharpness. To this end the company has to find new ways to innovate with the machinery they have available and within the constraints of the materials

they are working with. For the stoneware flooring Golem produces, firing in the enormous kiln can take up to 48 hours and when the tiles are superheated, they vitrify and become the most resistant ceramic building material after porcelain. They acquire a hardness that surpasses granite and a finish that is resistant to frost and acid, and that will develop its own natural patina over time. "In the 1850's Eugen von Boch developed the technique that made the production of polychrome stoneware floor tiles possible," Tomas adds.

"Until the 1920s those tiles were produced in large numbers in European countries, especially in Germany but in the years that followed, the technique passed into oblivion until Golem resurrected it in 1995, when we were commissioned with the reproduction of bi-colored stoneware tiles for the Karl-Borromäus Church in Vienna's Central Cemetery. We were the first company worldwide to practice this technique again; it was not easy at all, but we made it." •

A STAGGERING 80 PERCENT OF
THE WORK IN THE GOLEM
STUDIO IS STILL DONE BY HAND,
SIMPLY BECAUSE THERE IS NO
OTHER ALTERNATIVE.

left: Tile painting and creating
pillow paneling.

above: A building with glazed tiles by
Golem on Berlin's Europaplatz.

EL SOLITARIO
CUSTOM MOTORCYCLES

DAVID BORRAS IS AN ENFANT TERRIBLE OF THE CUSTOM MOTORBIKE WORLD. FROM HIS WORKSHOP IN GALICIA HE HANDCRAFTS EXAMPLES OF RIDEABLE ART THAT LOOK LIKE MONSTERS ON WHEELS.

David Borras, the visionary behind El Solitario MC, sees motorcycles as one of the last bastions of freedom. He left a successful career in finance and commodity trading to pursue his passion, and since 2010 has been manufacturing custom-made motorcycles out of Galicia in Spain. While most custom motorcycle builders work within the confines of a chosen theme and, like classical composers, create variations of that theme, El Solitario's bikes are only recognizable because they look like no other machine on two wheels.

Borras views each motorbike as a blank canvas onto which he projects his rock 'n' roll philosophy revolving around speed, relentless creativity, taking risks, and above all, freedom. To the outsider, there is no consistent thread to his motorcycles designs; however, all El Solitario motorcycles share a flamboyant signature style recognizable to motorcycle enthusiasts. David and his tight-knit team, consisting of a mechanic and a master metalworker, continually defy the constraints of traditional engineering with these Frankenstein-esque special creations. They produce meticulously crafted machines with a patchwork of parts until each motorcycle is a concrete expression of the El Solitario ethos. Valeria Libano, David Borras's wife and partner-in-crime, is behind the brand's motorcycle accessories and clothing products. The high-end gear is made following the same values of quality and originality, with materials including natural skins, raw selvedge denim, merino wool, and sterling silver. Together, Borras and

Libano have set new standards and created waves in the custom motorcycle scene.

An El Solitario motorcycle invariably displays completely new bodywork, as the only parts that remain from the donor bike are the frame and engine. Borras and his team take the time to develop a completely new concept for interpretation of the machine, sometimes adding unexpected components such as a second or even a third headlight, an outboard fuel tank, or old-school fishtail pipes. Each creation begins with a name and is given nothing short of a personality: there's Winning Loser, a low-slung 1985 Yamaha SR, Trimotoro, a sculptural 1985 Moto Guzzi V65, and Gonzo, a statuesque 1986 BMW R45. The most recent creation is Impostor, a simply outrageous 2014 BMW R9T that is lined with cage-like metalwork and whose tank has been engraved by a tattoo artist with the words of a ballad dating back to 1694. Borras explains that until now he conceived of all his motorcycles as women, but "Impostor is the first 'he'."

El Solitario motorcycles pair superb craftsmanship with loud design. Beauty and practicality do not interest David Borras as he seeks to challenge common perceptions of what a motorcycle can or should be. The only constraint is that the motorcycle has to be drivable—Borras calls it "rideable art." Even though he concedes that it sometimes takes a lot of energy to defend his craft that inevitably polarizes the bike world as "there are unwritten laws that you find out about when you step on them," it is undeniably worth the fight if it means pursuing his passion to the fullest. •

David Borras, the founder of El Solitario, working on one of his custom motorbikes.

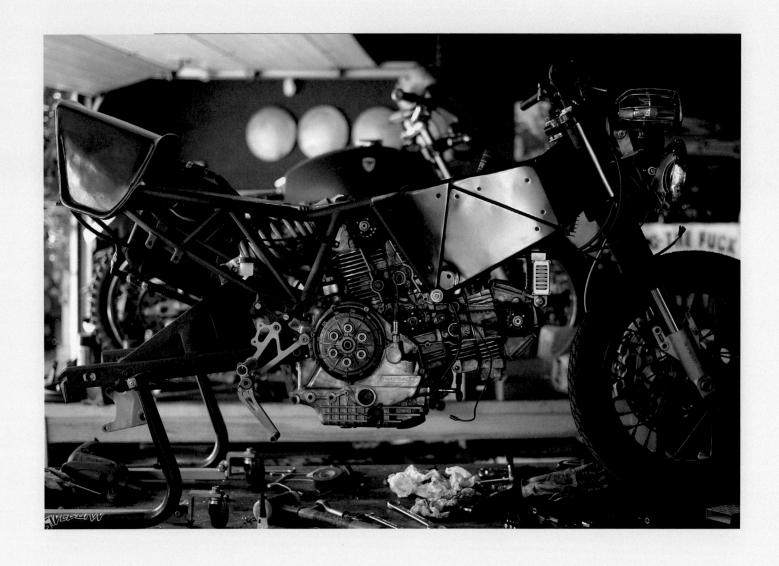

BORRAS VIEWS EACH MOTOR-
BIKE AS A BLANK CANVAS
ONTO WHICH HE PROJECTS
HIS ROCK'N'ROLL PHILOSOPHY
REVOLVING AROUND SPEED,
RELENTLESS CREATIVITY,
TAKING RISKS, AND ABOVE ALL,
FREEDOM.

above: El Solitario's
Petardo.

right: Casting belt buckles
at the shop.

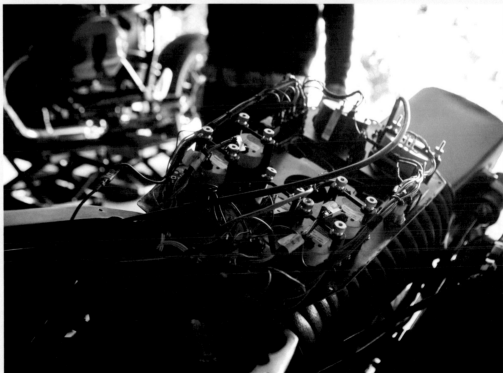

above left: El Solitario's
Impostor in its early stages.

right: Inside
El Solitario's Petardo.

El Solitario's
Baula motorcycle.

BEAUTY AND PRACTICALITY
DO NOT INTEREST DAVID BORRAS
AS HE SEEKS TO CHALLENGE
COMMON PERCEPTIONS OF WHAT A
MOTORCYCLE CAN OR SHOULD BE.

left: Maxwell Paternoster painting
Marrajo's tank and El Solitario's Baula
in the mock-up phase.

ABOUBAKAR FOFANA
TEXTILE DESIGNER

A FORMER CALLIGRAPHIC ARTIST, ABOUBAKAR FOFANA RETURNED TO HIS NATIVE MALI AFTER A SPELL IN FRANCE TO EXPLORE AND REVIVE THE COUNTRY'S RICH TEXTILE DYEING TRADITIONS.

Dividing his time between Paris and Bamako, Malian artist, calligrapher and master dyer Aboubakar Fofana creates 100% natural vegetable indigo and mineral mud-dyed textiles using a range of natural fabrics. He hand-dyes indigo textiles in ethereal blue shades, from very pale to very deep. Many of his pieces are also made from Malian-grown organic cotton, handspun and handwoven by local artisans to Fofana's specifications. His dyes come from a time-consuming and exacting traditional technique which uses living bacteria to extract pigment from the leaves of indigo-bearing plants indigenous to Mali and Guinea. Fofana's workshop produces cushion covers and bedspreads in shades of ecru, deep indigo or tie-dye patterns, as well as table runners, throws, and scarfs. He also teaches dyeing techniques and makes contemporary art installations, as well as traveling and demonstrating his craftsmanship worldwide.

Fofana was born in Mali, but has spent much of his life in France. He was first known for his exquisite calligraphy and for his commercial graphic design work, and his first exhibitions were calligraphic in nature. It was not until he returned to Mali that he realized that age-old dyeing and textile techniques were in danger of being forgotten. Committed to preserving and revitalizing Mali's nearly lost textile heritage and the tradition of natural vegetable indigo dyeing, he spent years reading, experimenting, and teaching himself as well as seeking out textile masters throughout West Africa. Receiving the prestigious Villa Médici grant in 2000, he further refined his skills studying for six months in Japan with a master silk dyer and weaver, and remains respectful of Japanese textile techniques and aesthetics. In Japan, he noted the similarities not only between West African and Japanese dyeing techniques, but also similarities in the spiritual approach to indigo dyeing and indigo cloth between Japanese Shinto and West African animism.

Fofana's work also utilizes other dyes such as Bogolan mineral mud dye, but indigo is by far the most challenging process to master. When working

Aboubakar Fofana
dyeing indigo

WHEN WORKING WITH NATURAL INDIGO DYE, THE DYE-VAT MUST BE TREATED LIKE A LIVING ORGANISM, AS IT CONTAINS BACTERIA WHOSE HEALTH MUST BE MONITORED DAILY AND WHICH NEED TO BE FED AND KEPT AT A CONSTANT TEMPERATURE AND PH BALANCE.

above: Indigo ombré linen gauze mosquito net tent.

top right: Indigo cotton skeins.

bottom right: Hemp indigo shawl and indigo ombré linen shawl.

with natural indigo dye, the dye vat must be treated like a living organism, as it contains bacteria whose health must be monitored daily and which need to be fed and kept at a constant temperature and pH balance. During this period, lasting between seven and ten days, the blue pigment which is captured in the green indigo leaves is made accessible by a process of reduction through bacterial activity. It is only after the vat has been successfully shepherded through this difficult stage that dyeing can begin, and even then, the vat can only be used for a limited time and then must be rested to allow the bacteria to regrow.

The challenge lies not only in growing the crucial bacteria needed to start the vat, but also the skill needed to keep them alive. The standard period for maintaining a vat is nine months but Fofana is often able to keep a vat alive for up to twelve months or longer, and it is right at the end of the vat's life cycle that he is able to produce the lightest and most ethereal blues, whilst the darkest blues come from

young, vigorous vats. Fofana elaborates, "All of the materials I use are absolutely integral to my process and to the finished product. They all come from the natural world and are, in one sense, alive–that is, they impart their own essence to the process and the products. I use a very ancient fermented indigo technique in which whole, crushed indigo leaves are fermented over a careful ten-day process that creates very vibrant blues. Similarly, the mud-dyes use mud from the Niger River, the colour comes from the iron in the mud reacting with a mordant which is made from a local plant, and the iron imparts not only color but heaviness, weight to the textile, giving it a beautiful drape. I use a lot of different natural textiles but my favorite by far is the organic handspun Malian cotton, which is strip-woven to the dimensions I need for each piece." •

HERITAGE-PARIS
BICYCLE WORKSHOP

BROUGHT TOGETHER BY A PASSION FOR FRANCE'S RICH CYCLING HERITAGE, CYRIL SAULNIER TEAMED UP WITH ALEX AND SIMON BILLARD AS WELL AS A GROUP OF FRENCH CRAFTSMEN TO OFFER ENTIRELY CUSTOMIZABLE, HANDMADE BIKES FROM THEIR PARIS WORKSHOP.

Heritage-Paris was founded three years ago by a group of friends brought together by their love of beautiful objects, and a desire to celebrate the illustrious spirit of French bicycle making. Cyril Saulnier, along with the Billard brothers—Alex and Simon—have made it their personal mission to gather around them a group of French craftsmen, including former racing cyclist-turned-frame maker Daniel Hanart, as well as painters, printers, and part makers with a view to promoting French craftsmanship at every stage of the manufacturing process.

Their original concept was to allow clients to customize and build a dream bike to their own specifications through a series of technical and aesthetic options accessed on the Heritage-Paris website. Every aspect of each bike is fully customizable, from the colours and paint type, to the saddle, handlebars and steel connectors. Once a bike is ordered and under construction, each individual stage of the building

and finishing process can be viewed by the customer, either in the workshop in person or online. This creates a unique connection between owner and object, and reveals the human element involved in building a bicycle from scratch, with the finished piece delivered in four to six weeks.

The bikes themselves are available for men and women, and crafted from Columbus Niobium steel, an exceptionally lightweight, rigid, and hardwearing alloy, which is designed to provide greater resistance to atmospheric corrosion than traditional carbon steels. Daniel Hanart takes responsibility for overseeing the hand-building of each frame, with an eye to the harmonious proportions and meticulous hand-welded joints, meaning that each individual bike really is a pièce de résistance. It was one of the founders' early beliefs that the bikes they produce should be able to be passed from one generation to the next, and to this end, they are issued with lifetime guarantees against

The Heritage-Paris H-001 fixed gear bicycle is made to measure.

ONCE A BIKE IS ORDERED
AND UNDER CONSTRUCTION,
EACH INDIVIDUAL STAGE
OF THE BUILDING AND
FINISHING PROCESS CAN
BE VIEWED BY THE CUSTOMER,
EITHER IN THE WORKSHOP
IN PERSON OR ONLINE.

left: This saddle is the result of a
collaboration between Brooks England
and Heritage-Paris.

above: Heritage-Paris H-005.

top left: The H-020 CLM is a time trial and triathlon bike with a Columbus Airplane Aero aluminum frame made to measure.

bottom left: Heritage-Paris and Melinda Gloss collaborated to create the H-010 CLM for Paris-based concept store Colette.

structural and manufacturing flaws. As a commitment to sustainability, the waste products from the workshop, including paint and metal scraps, are recycled and all the Heritage-Paris packaging is made from recycled cardboard.

IT WAS ONE OF THE FOUNDERS' EARLY BELIEFS THAT THE BIKES THEY PRODUCE SHOULD BE ABLE TO BE PASSED FROM ONE GENERATION TO THE NEXT.

After only three years, the boys have clocked up collaborations with the likes of Collette and Isabelle Marant and have begun to work on a co-branded saddle project with renowned British saddle maker Brooks England, meaning the saddles can be as unique as the frames. Personalization has been taken to the next level with one client requesting a leather-covered frame. In response, Heritage-Paris teamed up with the winner of France's Best Bookbinder award who clocked up more than 70 hours of painstaking work enveloping the frame in three different types of leather. For another special commission with a James Bond theme, the bike's forks were coated in 24-carat gold for Thomas Erber's Le Cabinet de Curiosités project.

Obviously these examples are at the extreme end of the spectrum, but it demonstrates a genuine commitment to the celebration of top-tier French craftsmanship. Since the word "bespoke" has become ubiquitous, and is often misused as a synonym for anything intended to be seen as luxurious, to see a young company that champions traditional, skilled manufacturing processes while embracing the possibilities of a digital infrastructure is a welcome sight. •

HERVÉ VAN DER STRAETEN
FURNITURE DESIGNER

RENOWNED FURNITURE AND JEWELRY DESIGNER HERVÉ VAN DER STRAETEN CREATES MODERN CLASSICS WITH HIS CELEBRATION OF LUXE MATERIALS AND CONTEMPORARY CRAFTSMANSHIP.

Hervé van der Straeten is a French modern, neo-baroque furniture, lighting and jewelry designer based in Paris. A purveyor of form, he first gained recognition for his jewelry collections for haute couture houses such as Yves Saint Laurent, Christian Lacroix, and Jean-Paul Gaultier in the late 1980s as well as the now iconic bottle for Christian Dior's perfume, J'adore, in 2005. Venturing into interior design in 1992, and applying his jewelry making skills to the creation of furniture, decorative objects, lighting, and mirrors, his focus is often on contrasting materials and distinct forms, a partnership between architecture and sculpture. He derives inspiration from the animal, the mineral, and the organic to astounding effect.

Van der Straeten's designs are contradictory and asymmetrical, at once heavy and light, austere but extravagant, smooth, textured, dark, and gleaming. Utilizing traditional artisanal techniques in a contemporary way, each is a striking creation. Educated at the École National des Beaux-Arts in Paris as a painter, his design process always starts with oversized sketches in his notebooks, favoring the carefree nature of the line first, and then letting the materials and techniques furnish the idea further. With every new design, this allows him to explore methods like marquetry or ironwork, and new materials such as gilt bronze, lacquer, precious woods, hammered metals or antiqued brass in the warm, glimmering tones that have become part of his signature.

In his own bronze and cabinet-making workshops in Bagnolet, outside Paris, he works with a team of twenty-five craftsmen—which he considers both a privilege and a responsibility—enabling the knowledge of their crafts to live on. Here, van der Straeten personally selects the materials and oversees the creation of his pieces, some taking weeks or months to complete, with his team testing and mastering new skills, materials, and their tolerances. He experiments

Designer Hervé van der Straeten working on a piece in his atelier.

VAN DER STRAETEN'S
DESIGNS ARE CONTRADIC-
TORY AND ASYMMETRICAL,
AT ONCE HEAVY AND LIGHT,
AUSTERE BUT EXTRAVA-
GANT, SMOOTH, TEXTURED,
DARK, AND GLEAMING.

above: The Pipe Show console
is made from tubes of polished
golden brass.

bottom right: Van der Straeten's
designs, such as Console Empilée,
are asymmetrical and seemingly
contradictory.

"MY WORK COMBINES A RADICAL FREEDOM OF EXPRESSION WITH AN EXTREMELY WELL-CRAFTED QUALITY OF EXECUTION."

above: Buffet Bondage is made of faded plum lacquered wood and golden-brown patinated bronze.

and spends hours trying, despite bruises or breaks, to find the balance that plays with the principles of suspension and gravity, giving each piece its own individual logic. Often using his jewelry as a testing ground for studying shapes, there are a few familiar forms present or echoed in both collections. "I follow every step as my collections are conceived within my own ateliers, in Paris where the finest craftsmen and cabinet makers elaborate my creations," he says. "They spend hundreds of hours developing and making each piece thanks to their renowned savoir-faire."

"As an independent designer, I gained international recognition for my furniture, lamp, and mirror designs, which now represent the core of my activity. My work combines a radical freedom of expression with an extremely well-crafted quality of execution. Clean lines, elegance, and a hybrid sense of design characterize my approach," he adds. His gallery on rue Ferdinand Duval features his own work alongside

other artists and interior designers. There you can view one of his favorite pieces, the Console Empilée, designed in 2003. "This piece is about the contrast between lacquered wood and bronze. Bronze is one of the first materials I used and it's still one of my favorites; it's noble and timeless thanks to its unique patina. Lacquer is another favored material, especially for its sensuality and softness. Therefore, the Console Empilée remains one of my favorite pieces: It's playful and seems nonchalant, but is in fact a precise architecture." Van der Straeten's furniture is collected by the Le Mobilier National, the official supplier of furnishings and decorative objects to the French state since Louis XIV, and in 2007, was awarded the Entreprise de Patrimoine Vivant, a national certification as a Living Heritage Company awarded by the French Ministry of Culture. •

RALEIGH DENIM WORKSHOP
JEANSMITHS

CELEBRATING THE ENDURING SPIRIT OF CLASSIC AMERICAN DENIM MANUFACTURERS, HUSBAND-AND-WIFE TEAM SARAH YARBOROUGH AND VICTOR LYTVINENKO PRODUCE SMALL BATCHES OF JEANS AND OTHER CLOTHING FROM THEIR HOMETOWN OF RALEIGH, NORTH CAROLINA.

Raleigh Denim Workshop is a small-batch, hand-crafted American denim brand produced by husband-and-wife team Sarah Yarborough and Victor Lytvinenko, alongside their team of jeansmiths in their hometown of Raleigh, North Carolina. Founded in 2007, the company uses denim produced by Cone Mills White Oak, one of the oldest American mills, which opened in 1905. Made on shuttle looms from the 1920s and 1930s, the denim is produced with milled organic cotton in the historical heart of America's jeans making territory. Fascinated with the golden era of manufacturing after Second World War, Sarah and Victor set out to learn the skills their grandparents grew up with.

Recently accepted into the Council of Fashion Designers of America, the founders learned the traditional techniques of jeans production after acquiring the former workshop and denim workers of the last Levi's factory in Bakersville, as well as patternmakers and mechanics from around the state. Marrying old-school-methods with modern fits, their early success allowed them to expand into men's and women's collections, all produced in the United States with a focus on design, process, materials, and craftsmanship.

Working closely with the mill at every stage of the process, from the sourcing of the cotton, the twist of the fiber, the different shades of the dye to the weight of the fabrics, the patterns of the jeans are created primarily by their 78-year-old patternmaker who worked for Levi's and has over fifty years of experience. Each pair of jeans is hand-stitched, labeled with an edition number, and signed by either Victor, Sarah, or one of their technicians in their workshop at 319, Martin Street. Their first big order came from legendary department store Barneys New York in 2008 for 114 pairs of jeans. They didn't have the funds to purchase all the

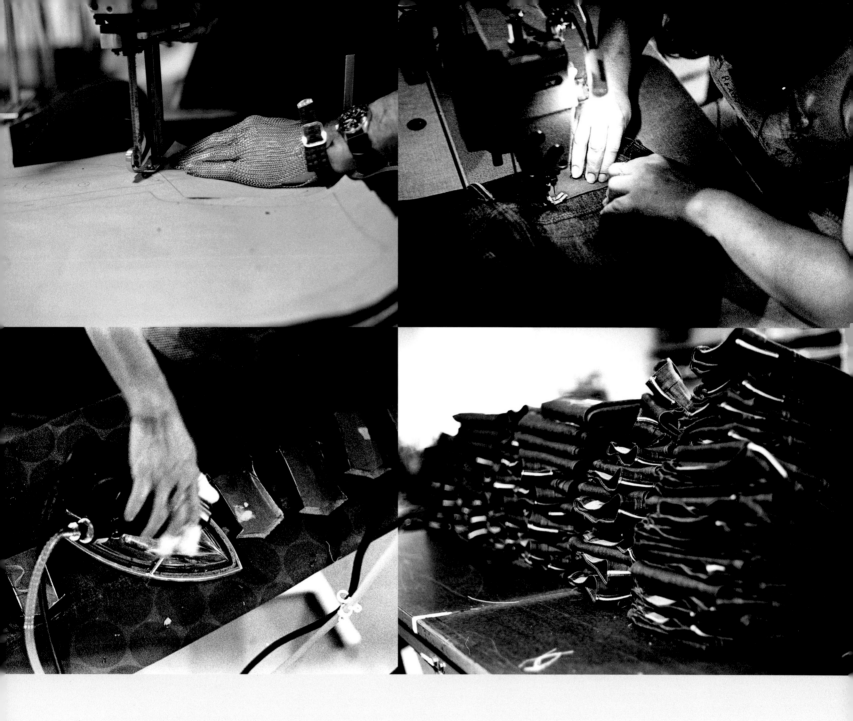

material they needed to fulfill the order until luckily an economic stimulus package helped them and, since then, the company has gone from strength to strength.

MEN'S AND WOMEN'S COLLECTIONS, ALL PRODUCED IN THE UNITED STATES WITH A FOCUS ON DESIGN, PROCESS, MATERIALS, AND CRAFTSMANSHIP.

left: Raleigh Designers Sarah Yarborough and Victor Lytvinenko in the workshop.

above: Raleigh Jeans are hand-sewn, labeled with an edition number, and signed by the designers.

"We're naturally drawn to objects that have a story or a history we can relate to and appreciate. We're also interested in things that belong to a particular area and reflect a specific culture," they say. "We think that these things are much of what makes a garment or an object remarkable. So we produce in the USA, using specialized vintage sewing machines—our hemming machine is the original hemming machine from the 1930s. We draft our patterns by hand, and cut and sew in small batches, and we number and sign each pair. We do all of these things in order to make a garment that speaks about where it's from and how it came to be as soon as you pick it up. Those are the kinds of clothes we like to wear."

The Curatory is Raleigh's multi-brand store in the front of their workshop where they mix their jeans with names such as Nash, Wilkes, Camden, and Union, alongside things they have picked up on their travels, from clothing to gifts and stationary. A 40-foot window runs along the front of the store so passersby can watch the denim production as it happens. In the autumn of 2012, Raleigh opened their first store on Elizabeth Street in New York's NoLita shopping district. •

A. LANGE & SÖHNE
WATCHMAKER

A RENOWNED WATCHMAKER THAT WAS ABANDONED WHEN ITS ASSETS WERE SEIZED BY THE SOVIET ADMINISTRATION FOLLOWING WWII, THE HOUSE WAS BROUGHT BACK TO LIFE BY THE FOUNDER'S GREAT-GRANDSON, TAKING THE WATCHMAKING INDUSTRY BY STORM.

The fine watchmaking world is notoriously obsessed with pedigree. And why shouldn't it be? When each individual aspect of this highly specialized and intricate craft can take many years to master, and some of the major houses have been operating more or less continuously (save, perhaps, for a change of ownership or two) for more than a century. This makes it all the more remarkable that A. Lange & Söhne has only been open for business in its modern iteration since 1990.

Of course that's not quite the whole story—the Lange house was founded in 1845 by Ferdinand A. Lange in the remote township of Glashütte, Saxony, in the east of Germany. The company was renowned for high-quality pocket watches, but after World War II, the Soviet administration confiscated the company, seizing its assets, and the brand A. Lange & Söhne was abandoned. In 1990, the founder's great grandson, Walter Lange, revived the company. Four years later, he presented its first collection of wristwatches in more than 40 years, which garnered great acclaim. Since 2000, it has been part of the Richemont conglomerate since 2000, A. Lange & Söhne has gone from strength to strength. Lange CEO Wilhelm Schmid comments, "The main challenge was to find a convincing answer to the question: What would an A. Lange & Söhne watch look like if the brand had not been discontinued for more than forty years due to the political upheavals in post-war Germany? With an equally bold and ingenious concept the team around Walter Lange managed to come up with a breathtaking first collection—a fresh innovative reinterpretation of the brand that made it attractive for today's audience."

Another phenomenon of the contemporary watchmaking landscape is the feeling that, at times, bigger watches and more extreme designs are necessary to establish market share. A. Lange & Söhne is a refreshing exception to this rule. The watches themselves are deeply restrained, bordering on the conservative, but with an almost imperceptible harmony of proportion that begs the viewer to take a closer look. Decentralized dial designs, outsized date windows and an overall feeling of refined elegance create an impression that is at once classic and surprisingly modern. The watches themselves are crafted exclusively from precious metals (there were a few rare steel examples in the first years) and all the components of a Lange watch are developed, produced, and assembled in-house at their Glashütte manufacture. The decoration steps away from the exuberance of traditional Swiss finishing techniques in favor of a more sober German approach with three-quarter plates and a distinctive undulating ribbing pattern known as Glashütte Stripes. In addition, the balance cock of each watch is engraved by hand, carrying the individual style of the person who worked on it. The

The A. Lange & Söhne Zeitwerk Handwerkskunst is a modern marvel, regularly appearing at the top of collectors' lists of favorite pieces

left: Each watch is assembled twice to guarantee the standards of quality that A. Lange & Söhne require.

The mirror-smooth surface of the watch is achieved by rubbing it in a figure-of-eight motion with special foils coated with diamond dust.

framework of the movements is constructed from an alloy called German silver (actually an alloy of nickel, copper, and zinc), which gives components a delicate luminescence when compared to the brighter plated brass usually used in Switzerland. "For a manufactory that relies on ingenuity and craftsmanship the human element is the cornerstone of success," says Wilhelm. "Therefore, we look for the best employees, invest in their training, and continuously improve their working conditions. The positive effects are felt daily: Working with quality as our only measure, our watchmakers are driven by their passion and the ambition to build the world's best watches." While the finishing and construction of each watch places A. Lange & Söhne squarely among the best watchmakers in the world, there is also a technical side to the house that is worthy of mention. The continual pursuit of greater accuracy, better energy efficiency, and improved legibility are constant preoccupations that pervade everything A. Lange & Söhne does. A particularly

"WORKING WITH QUALITY AS OUR ONLY MEASURE, OUR WATCHMAKERS ARE DRIVEN BY THEIR PASSION AND THE AMBITION TO BUILD THE WORLD'S BEST WATCHES."

notable example is the remarkable Lange Zeitwerk Handwerkunst, produced in a limited edition of just 30 pieces. Featuring Lange's unique "mechanical digital" display, the black-rhodiumed white gold dial features a tremblage engraving, an escapement constructed in hardened 18-carat gold, and a beautifully hand-engraved movement. Of course there are very significant Lange Grand Complication timepieces that win awards and break new ground, but it's the obsession with these technical aspects in every watch they produce, in addition to the fact they have achieved so much in the short time since the house was re-established, that makes A. Lange & Söhne so exceptional. •

E15
INTERIOR DESIGN

**ARCHITECT AND DESIGNER PHILIPP MAINZER FOUNDED E15 IN 1995
AND NAMED IT AFTER THE STUDIO'S EAST LONDON POSTCODE.
TODAY THE PRACTICE EXPLORES THE RELATIONSHIP BETWEEN CUT-
TING-EDGE TECHNOLOGICAL PROCESSES AND TRADITIONAL
CRAFTING TECHNIQUES IN FURNITURE AND INDUSTRIAL DESIGN.**

Named after the postcode of his first studio in East London, architect and designer Philipp Mainzer founded e15 in 1995. An alumnus of Central Saint Martins and the Architecture Association, he has received international recognition for his furniture designs, as well as his innovative approach to creating spaces.

Originally renowned for working with solid wood construction techniques, in recent years, Philipp and his team have branched out and signature elements now include playful use of color, juxtaposition of luxurious and utilitarian materials as well as experimenting with proportion. e15's designs trace an interesting line between high-grade materials, cutting-edge technological processes and handcrafted production methods. "Simplicity, craftsmanship, and pure use of the material were the founding principles of e15, says Philipp. "We started in 1995 with the design of five solid wood tables in European oak, including the much recognized Bigfoot table. At this time, slick, minimalist design was in fashion; however, we felt a strong need to feature solid wood in its purest form, even exposing the unique natural cracks and knots in the timber.

**THE STUDIO TRAVERSES
DIFFERING CREATIVE GENRES
IN AN EFFORTLESS WAY.**

Working closely with a regular team of designers, architects, and artists, Phillip promotes an "open approach to diverse cultures and disciplines." The studio traverses differing creative genres in an effortless way, and is now represented in more than 40 countries around the world. "The human element is central to the look and appeal of our products," he continues. "For example, in our hand-knotted Kavir carpets we feature the fringes in contrasting shades

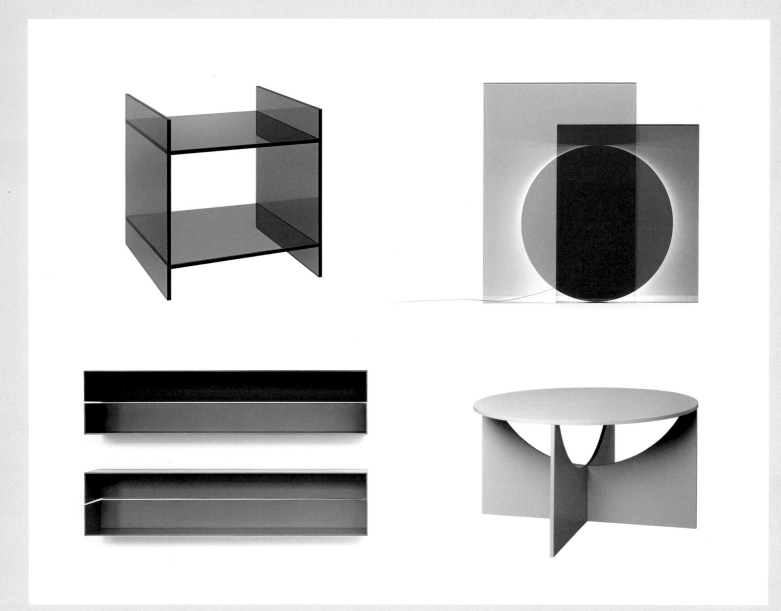

to highlight the human hands that knotted the carpet as opposed to a machine. Ironically, in most modern carpets the fringe is omitted, as if to erase the human aspect of the product. Our Habibi trays made with pure brass, copper, or stainless steel are hand-finished and polished, amongst other examples. Some of the small workshops that we work with are social cooperatives, such as Teixidors in Spain, who produce the blanket Cuadro."

One of e15's most emblematic pieces is the Backenzahn side table, which has become something of a symbol for the company, and sits in the permanent collections of several museums around the world. The table (which can also be used as a stool) is constructed from four legs, which fit together snugly to create the top surface. The tapering legs and incisions on the sides ensure that even after the piece is assembled, the constituent parts are still visible. The overall impression is one of strength, with an

emphasis on integrity of materials and honesty of construction. "With our close attention to the high quality of manufacturing," Philipp concludes, "We

"WE HOPE TO CONTRIBUTE TO THE PRESERVATION AND FURTHER DEVELOPMENT OF TRADITIONAL CRAFT PROFESSIONS AND HELP TO BRING THEM UP TO DATE."

hope to contribute to the preservation and further development of traditional craft professions and help to bring them up to date. Traditional wood joining techniques such as dovetails for our tables, modern laser cutting, and bending aluminum for lights, and hand-finishing most of our products are central to our design philosophy." •

left clockwise: Glass table CT07 DREI, floor Lamp LT04 COLOUR, coffee table FK05 CHARLOTTE, and shelf SH06 PROFIL.

above: Designer and co-founder of e15, Philipp Mainzer.

left: Table legs for e15's
Bigfoot dining table, considered
a design classic.

right: Nota is a fold-down writing
desk by Elisabeth Lux with sliding
storage compartments that
can be rearranged or removed.

LOBMEYR
GLASSMAKER

A PIONEER OF AUSTRIAN GLASSMAKING AT ITS BEST, LOBMEYR HAS ALWAYS FOSTERED A STRONG CULTURE OF COLLABORATION WITH ARTISTS AND DESIGNERS, AS WELL AS ENSURING THAT ITS RARE AND SPECIALIZED CRAFT TECHNIQUES ARE KEPT ALIVE FOR THE NEXT GENERATION.

Founded in 1823, Lobmeyr is one of the most pioneering and respected names in Austrian glassmaking. Over the course of six generations, the family company has pushed the boundaries of what can be done with this remarkable material and contributed to our enduring fascination with its lustrous appeal. The manufacture became purveyors to royalty, garnered great acclaim at the world fairs, and in 1883 delivered the world's first electric chandelier to Vienna's Imperial Palace, cementing its reputation as a leader at the forefront of innovation.

Preferring a "subtle shine over loud glitter," the Lobmeyr style is one of delicate, hand-blown shapes, subtle curves, and unostentatious elegance. With a strong tradition in collaborating with artists and designers, the Lobmeyr archive contains many pieces now considered to be design classics, which are featured in permanent museum collections around the world, including MoMA in New York. Painters, sculptors, and architects have all been invited to

design for Lobmeyr, and there was a particularly close tie to the craftspeople of the Wiener Werkstätte [Vienna Workshops] community of visual artists at the beginning of the 20th century, leading to modern designs that were a radical departure from the historical references that had gone before. From the likes of Josef Hoffmann and Adolf Loos a century ago to contemporary designers including Mark Braun and Tomás Alonso, the house continues in this spirit of collaboration today.

One of the Lobmeyr signatures is known as "Muslin Glass"—crystal blown to a thickness of only 0.7 mm, creating a uniquely delicate connection between the glass and the drinker. Only the most experienced glassblowers can execute pieces in this unique way. Because glass cools much more quickly when it's blown so thin, they must also increase the speed and assertiveness with which they work. Despite the fact that it's so delicate to the touch, Muslin glass is actually remarkably durable owing

Lobmeyr is in its sixth generation as a family business and is run by Leonid, Johannes, and Andreas Rath.

above: The Lobmeyr glass creators traditionally come from a wide range of backgrounds; they are painters, architects and designers.

The drinking glasses Seven Deadly Sins—Seven Heavenly Virtues are designed by renowned Austrian designer Stefan Sagmeister.

to the inner elasticity of the material, and a single glass made in this way will pass through at least 24 pairs of hands during its creation, undergoing four quality inspections, the last of which is always by a member of the founding family.

PREFERRING A "SUBTLE SHINE OVER LOUD GLITTER," THE LOBMEYR STYLE IS ONE OF DELICATE, HAND-BLOWN SHAPES, SUBTLE CURVES, AND UNOSTENTATIOUS ELEGANCE.

Lobmeyr is known for intricate detailing and engraving techniques of the kind that would have been common during the last century but today are much harder to come by. Today the firm has been known to incorporate one-man workshops that are on the verge of closing, including their machinery and tools, in order to save the techniques from being lost. One recent example is the collaboration with a craftsman who specializes in the French bronzes of Versailles, which Lobmeyr was unable to produce before, but can now incorporate into future designs. The combination of this kind of craft at the highest level, coupled with an openness to collaboration and a pursuit of innovative design has served Lobmeyr well in its long history. Striving for designs that are at once novel and enduring, the style of the house is as relevant today as it will be in years to come. •

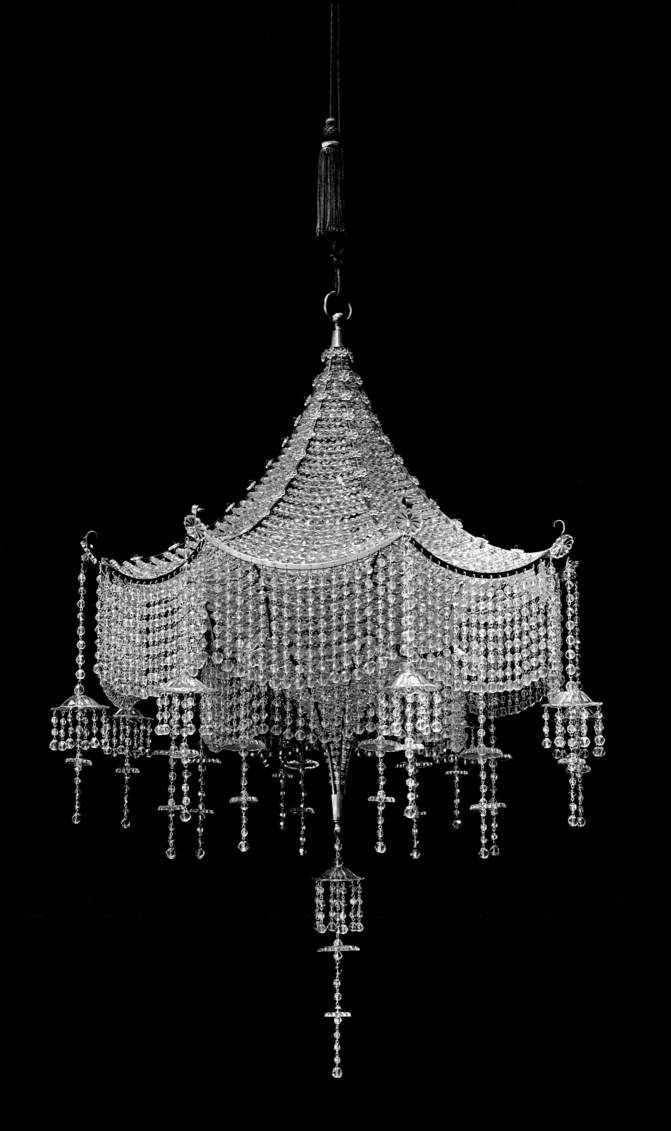

THE COMBINATION OF THIS KIND
OF CRAFT AT THE HIGHEST
LEVEL, COUPLED WITH AN OPEN-
NESS TO COLLABORATION AND
A PURSUIT OF INNOVATIVE
DESIGN HAS SERVED LOBMEYR
WELL IN ITS LONG HISTORY.

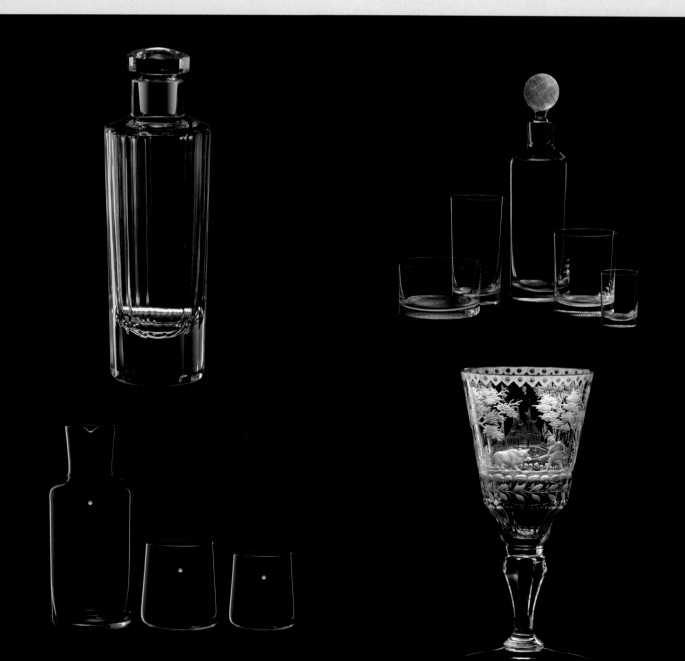

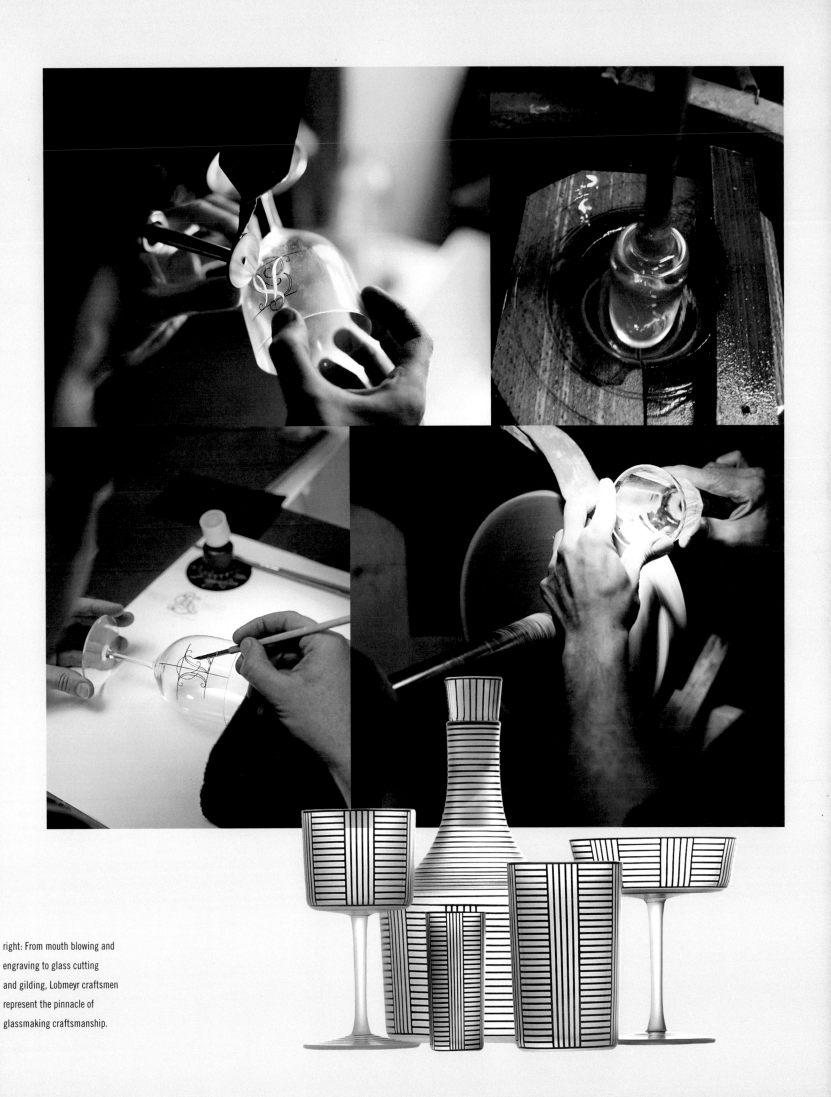

right: From mouth blowing and engraving to glass cutting and gilding, Lobmeyr craftsmen represent the pinnacle of glassmaking craftsmanship.

SHINOLA
URBAN GOODS MANUFACTURE

TAKING ITS NAME FROM THE DEFUNCT SHOE POLISH BRAND, SHINOLA IS A WATCH, BICYCLE, AND LEATHER GOODS COMPANY BASED IN DETROIT THAT CHAMPIONS THE SPIRIT OF AMERICAN MANUFACTURING WHILE PARTICIPATING IN THE REJUVENATION OF THE BELEAGUERED CITY.

As the beating heart of America's automotive industry, the city of Detroit was made great by companies like Ford and General Motors, and by the thousands of workers who flocked to the city during a period of intense growth in the first half of the twentieth century. Since then, it has been well documented that Detroit has faced severe financial difficulties (filing for bankruptcy in July 2013 in the largest municipal collapse in US history), urban decay, and a mass exodus of the population, but among the green shoots of recovery that have started to appear in recent years, Shinola is a notable example. The Shinola name was better known in the US as a shoe polish brand that was popular until the 1970s and has since passed into obscurity. The trademark was available, and has been recently revived by Tom Kartsotis, founder of Fossil Watches, as a new kind of American manufacturing company.

Detroit is home to some of the finest examples of industrial art deco architecture in the United States, a style that recalls the optimism, speed, and power of the golden age of manufacturing. The imposing Argonaut Building, once a research laboratory for General Motors, has recently been restored, in part by Shinola for use as a corporate headquarters and factory. Today they produce hand-built bicycles, watches, and leather goods in the space, and apart from a few exceptions (including Swiss watch components), all of Shinola's products are produced in the United States, and for the most part assembled in their Detroit factory. There has been a committed drive to recruit and employ local people in a city with one of the highest rates of unemployment in the country. Veteran watchmakers were brought in from Ronda, a Swiss watch manufacturer who is producing watch movements for Shinola, in order to train the

A watchmaker at Shinola's Detroit factory.

NO US WATCHMAKER HAS
PRODUCED WATCHES ON THIS
SCALE SINCE THE 1960s,
AND IT'S THIS PARTICULAR
NOTION OF "SKILL AT SCALE"
THAT IS AT THE HEART OF THE
SHINOLA ETHOS.

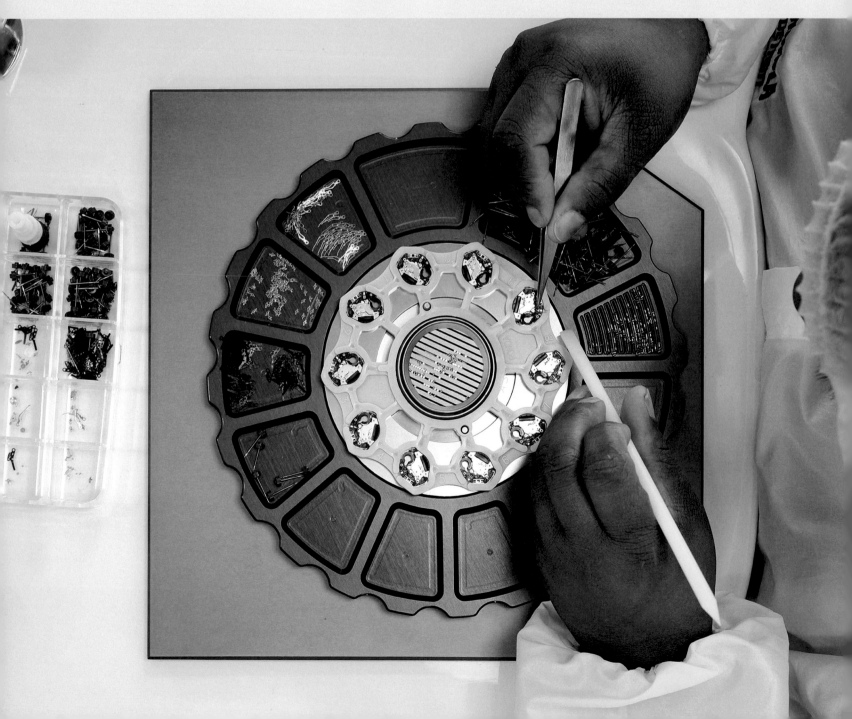

left: Shinola is the first company in decades to manufacture watches at this scale in the United States.

above: The Runwell model is the result of two years of work by multiple suppliers and designers.

new staff, none of whom had any prior watchmaking experience. No US watchmaker has produced watches on this scale since the 1960s, and it's this particular notion of "skill at scale" that is at the heart of the Shinola ethos.

Chicago's last leather tannery, Horween, supplies the vegetable-tanned leather for Shinola products, which are then sewn into watchstraps and other leather goods by Eric Scott, a small manufacturer in Missouri. Sourced from sustainably managed North American forests, the special paper for the Shinola journals is supplied by Edward Brothers Malloy, a family-owned company in Ann Arbor. Bicycle components are made by Waterford Precision Cycles in Wisconsin, and shipped to the Shinola site in Detroit

for assembly. The company is transparent about which elements of its products are still sourced from outside the USA, and is working all the time to reduce this number.

Although the products offered differ significantly from the original brand, it's the spirit of American manufacturing that lives on in Shinola today. It's an enormous feat to train large numbers of inexperienced recruits and turn them into skilled craftspeople in such a highly technical and specialized industry, but one that couldn't have come at a better time for the city. This idea that industry and manufacturing can be beautiful on a human as well as an aesthetic level is something to be commended. •

SHINOLA
DETROIT

BROWN
SHOE POLISH

NET WT. 4 OZ (112 G)

Shinola's bike designer
Sky Yaeger is an innovative
industry veteran.

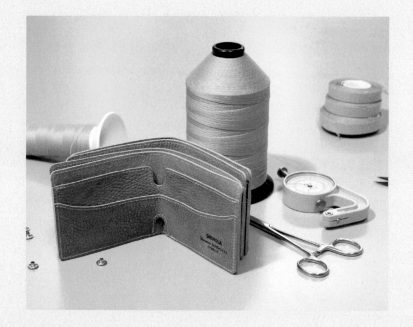

ALTHOUGH THE PRODUCTS OFFERED DIFFER SIGNIFICANTLY FROM THE ORIGINAL BRAND, IT'S THE SPIRIT OF AMERICAN MANUFACTURING THAT LIVES ON IN SHINOLA TODAY.

BULY 1803 PHARMACY

AN ESTEEMED 19TH-CENTURY PARISIAN PHARMACY, BROUGHT BACK TO LIFE BY ENTREPRENEUR RAMDANE TOUHAMI, WHO HAS SCOURED THE GLOBE IN SEARCH OF TRADITIONAL BEAUTY SECRETS FROM THE AMAZON TO THE AFRICAN PLAINS AND BEYOND.

The story of perfume and cosmetics company Buly, begins in 1803 on rue Saint-Honoré in Paris where Jean-Vincent Bully established a distillery placing himself at the vanguard of a new era for beauty. It was an age when perfumers were still the heirs of the master craftsmen from the Ancien Régime, while drawing from new science and technology to perfect their products. He quickly gained notoriety for his signature scented skincare vinegars and even inspired Honoré de Balzac's protagonist character César Birotteau in "Scènes de la vie Parisienne" in *La Comédie Humaine.*

After successfully relaunching and then selling royal wax manufacturer Cire Trudon, established in 1643, as a candle and fragrance house in 2011, French-Moroccan entrepreneur Ramdane Touhami was on the hunt for another "new legend" that he could transform into a global business. After touring around 130 old apothecaries and *officines* with histories ranging from the 15th to the 19th centuries, he came across the Bully archives at Les Archives Départementales de la Seine and realized he had found exactly what he was looking for.

Wanting to create a universal trading post for beauty secrets amassed over the centuries, his idea was to unearth potions and cosmetics from around the globe. Today, Buly1803 sells one of the world's most complete collections of beauty oils, perfumes, tinctures, and clays from places as secluded as the Amazonian rainforest from remote tribes in Africa. In a sense, Ramdane explains, Bully was one of the inventors of modern cosmetics and perfumery, and he was fascinated with the number of references listed in his catalogs for lotions, vinegars, hydrating soaps, creams, powders, ointments, and perfumes.

BULY1803 SELLS ONE OF THE WORLD'S MOST COMPLETE COLLECTIONS OF BEAUTY OILS, PERFUMES, TINCTURES AND CLAYS FROM PLACES AS REMOTE AS THE AMAZONIAN FOREST AND REMOTE TRIBES IN AFRICA.

Faithful to Bully's original recipes, he has developed products that comply with today's stringent regulations yet build on the formulas of old cosmetics when they were free of parabens, phenoxyethanol and silicones. The products comply with today's stringent regulations, all the while retaining an old

The beauty brand was resurrected after Ramdane Touhami and Victoire de Taillac discovered the Bully archives, founded by Parisian perfumer Jean-Vincent Bully in 1803.

THE PRODUCTS COMPLY WITH
TODAY'S STRINGENT
REGULATIONS, ALL THE WHILE
RETAINING AN OLD WORLD
ELEGANCE AND EMPHASIS
ON NATURAL INGREDIENTS.

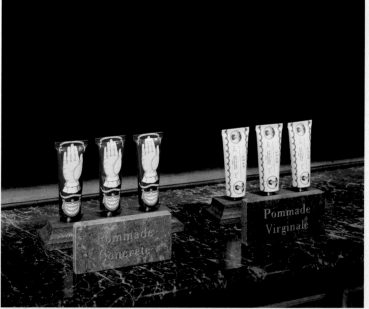

left: L'Officine Universelle
Buly counts more than 400 products
among its inventory.

above: The interior of the store is
inspired by an old apothecary
shop and has been faithfully restored
in the style of the 19th century.

world elegance and emphasis on natural ingredients. "For example, since the dawn of time, man has been nurtured by beauty oils," says Ramdane. "Each region of the world boasts oils derived from indigenous plants, which are often naturally suited to the needs of the skin and hair of the people who hail from the same soil. L'Officine Universelle Buly knows their properties, and selects and recommends these precious oils for their unique cosmetic benefits. Picking only virgin oils and macerates, either cold-pressed or obtained through other gentle maceration and extraction methods, the seeds, fruits, flowers, and stems from which they are extracted have been treated delicately and only once, without resorting to any heat or chemical treatment. Thus, once filtered, they can better preserve the full vigor of their virtues.

They must be carefully stored in a dark and temperate environment in order to retain their stability and effectiveness." Working closely with skilled workers from the region, their suppliers "are the front-line ambassadors of the craft industry of cosmetics."

Offering 15 product lines and over 400 products, the flagship store at 6 rue Bonaparte on the Left Bank displays authentic 19th-century apothecary décor—painted white and blue ceilings, turquoise and cream enameled terracotta tiles from Etruscan stoves covering the floor, cabinets clad in gnarled elm, burned walnut, and oak cover three of the walls, and the countertops are made of Bénou marble, perfectly capturing the spirit and mood of the company and the era. •

PIERRE FREY
FABRICS MANUFACTURER

A FAMILY-OWNED FABRIC AND FURNISHING COMPANY, PIERRE FREY PRODUCES A WIDE RANGE OF WHIMSICAL DESIGNS UNDER THE COMPANY'S OWN BRAND, AS WELL AS A SERIES OF SPECIALIZED SUBSIDIARIES.

La maison Pierre Frey, founded in 1935, is a family-owned fabric and furnishing house with a proud heritage of designing, creating, and manufacturing fabrics and wallpapers in the French tradition. The company's collection includes more than 7,000 styles, comprising not only the Pierre Frey designs and homeware collection, but also the collections from the company's three other brands: Braquenié, Fadini Borghi, and Boussac.

In 1972, founder Pierre Frey entrusted the company's creative direction to his son Patrick who was 29 years old at the time. Today, with a profound sense of French savoir-faire and savoir-vivre, Patrick draws his inspiration for patterns from such diverse locales as imperial China, 18th-century France, and contemporary Africa. A new fabric always begins with Patrick's eclectic interpretation of a particular style, as he maintains that, "the important thing is, above all, never listen to other people." When his vision for a new fabric is complete he enlists his draftsmen to bring it to life, each model relying on a mastery of line and color. He knows from experience which draftsman will be best suited to produce which pattern, as each comes with its own unique challenges.

This also relates to questions of fabric type, and these can range from cotton to taffetas to linen, and whether to print, embroider or weave the motif to best allow the composition to sing. The creation of a fabric demands the involvement of a whole team but at every stage of the process Patrick is responsible for the final decision. Since 1961, 70 percent of their collections have been made at the company's own fabric factory in northern France, that recently received the French Living Heritage award.

WITH A PROFOUND SENSE OF FRENCH SAVOIR-FAIRE AND SAVOIR-VIVRE, PATRICK DRAWS HIS PATTERN INSPIRATIONS FROM SUCH DIVERSE LOCALES AS IMPERIAL CHINA, 18TH-CENTURY FRANCE, AND CONTEMPORARY AFRICA.

In 1991, as part of an expansion strategy for the company in order to diversify their offering, Maison Pierre Frey acquired the French fabric house Braquenié, founded in 1824. Having adorned the

Patrick Frey, son of the founder Pierre Frey, took over the business in 1972.

right: The company's collection includes more than 7,000 styles of fabrics.

Louvre, the Vatican, all the courts of Europe under Napoléon III as well as Victor Hugo's house, and best known for its Indian fabrics, toiles de Jouy, and hand-knotted carpets–,Braquenié represents the best of cotton fabrics. In 2004, the textile brands Fadini Borghi and Boussac joined the family. Fadini Borghi, with a nod to the spirit of Italy, specializes in silks like voided velvets, taffetas, damasks, lampas, and brocades inspired by 16th to 19th-century Italian motifs, art deco, and contemporary patterns. Meanwhile Boussac, founded in 1933, offers technical fabrics with qualities such as resistance to wear, light, and fire. "My father is the head of the studio, he decides the theme of each collection. Next January one of the themes is Aboriginal and another one is Napoleon III. This is the beauty of having five brands with totally

different identities. The starting point could be a painting, a picture, a drawing, an idea, a sample, or he could be inspired by something from his everyday life," comments Patrick, and the brand ambassador of the house, also called Pierre.

Beyond this, Maison Pierre Frey owns a remarkable collection of 30,000 documents on designs, fabrics, and carpet samples dating back to the 16th century, which is based in Paris and can be searched by period, color, motif, or technique. The archive is a resource that makes the company the point of contact for museums and dealers all over the world. This set-up in combination with the specialist houses for different fabrics allows La Maison Pierre Frey to stay at the epicenter of world fabrics and design innovation. •

MAISON PIERRE FREY OWNS A
REMARKABLE COLLECTION OF
30,000 DOCUMENTS ON DESIGNS,
FABRICS, AND CARPET SAMPLES,
DATING BACK TO THE 16TH CEN-
TURY, WHICH IS BASED IN PARIS.

right: Pierre Frey is traditionally
a fabric and furnishing house, but is
open to contemporary ideas,
which has led to the creation of home
accessories and furniture collections.

above: Pierre Frey preserves its
remarkable heritage and actively
archives designs from the company's
four brands along with a selection
of rare pieces acquired at
auctions, from antique dealers,
as well as from private collections.

right: Braquenié carpets and rugs
are made in Pierre Frey's workshop
where the widths are assembled
manually by craftsmen using
traditional techniques.

MAST BROTHERS
CHOCOLATE MAKERS

BROTHERS RICK AND MICHAEL MAST RUN A BEAN-TO-BAR CHOCOLATE FACTORY IN WILLIAMSBURG, BROOKLYN THAT FOR THE LAST FEW YEARS HAS BEEN AT THE VANGUARD OF A RENEWED INTEREST IN AMERICAN ARTISANAL FOOD PRODUCTION.

The bearded brothers behind Mast Brothers Chocolate, Rick and Michael Mast.

Rick and Michael Mast, the impressively bearded duo behind Mast Brothers Chocolate, have created something of a revolution in American craft chocolate manufacture in the last few years. Everything from "bean to bar" is done in their Williamsburg factory—from sourcing, sorting, roasting, winnowing, grinding, and tempering the chocolate, and then wrapping it in the almost too-good-to-be-true packaging. Since 2007, the company has grown to 50 employees, but they still approach the process with the same small-batch mentality and artisanal attention to detail as when they were just starting out in their apartment.

Mast Brothers chocolate is crafted using only two ingredients: cacao and cane sugar. The brothers source the finest cacao available from countries such as Belize, Madagascar, Papua New Guinea, and the Dominican Republic, and they are active in

supporting small farms and cooperatives in pursuit of their raw ingredients, something they feel makes a tangible difference to the end result.

Cocoa beans are picked from trees in pods, at which point they resemble a white fruit with a pulpy texture. The beans are dried and fermented by the farmers and, by the time they arrive in the US, they are ready for roasting. All of the beans the Mast Brothers use are roasted at their Brooklyn factory in convection ovens. After the roasting process, the husks are removed using a winnower machine, which separates the useable cocoa nibs from their husks. The newly separated nibs are then ground in stone grinders while sugar is added, and after 48 to 72 hours they are transformed into a silky chocolate paste. Like some wines, chocolate benefits from aging to allow the flavor profiles to develop and mature, and this

MAST BROTHERS
· Dark Chocolate ·
Brooklyn Blend
2.5 oz

left: The artisanal chocolate factory creates bean-to-bar handmade sweets in small batches and elaborate flavors.

above: Each bar is hand-wrapped with custom-designed paper in Brooklyn. The Mast Brothers source their cacao from small farms in Ecuador, Madagascar, and Venezuela.

takes from one to three months. After the chocolate has aged, it's melted down again and at this stage, an additional flavor can be added like sea salt or maple syrup. The chocolate is then poured in to molds and then it's ready for wrapping. Also worthy of note are the whimsical, patterned wrapper designs, created in-house and printed locally in Long Island City. They add to the sense of childlike wonder that comes from opening a weighty new bar of chocolate and breaking the golden foil—perhaps the only thing these bars have in common with a certain Mr. Wonka.

In the space of a few short years, the Mast Brothers operation has expanded significantly, and their product has become synonymous not only with an increased interest in craft chocolate, but also in artisan food production in a wider sense. The brothers have collaborated with a number of notable local businesses including the acclaimed Wythe Hotel in

THEIR PRODUCT HAS BECOME SYNONYMOUS NOT ONLY WITH AN INCREASED INTEREST IN CRAFT CHOCOLATE, BUT ALSO IN ARTISAN FOOD PRODUCTION IN A WIDER SENSE.

Brooklyn, as well as seeing their chocolate used in some of the most celebrated restaurant kitchens in America, including Thomas Keller's Per Se and Le Bernardin. Last year they also launched a cookbook titled *Mast Brothers Chocolate: A Family Cookbook*, which features not only traditional chocolate making recipes, but also ideas for cooking with chocolate including new favorites like Cocoa Coq au Vin. •

MÜHLBAUER
MILLINER

FOUNDED IN 1903 AS A MILLINERY WORKSHOP IN VIENNA, MÜHLBAUER HAD SOMEWHAT LOST ITS WAY WHEN FOURTH GENERATION SIBLINGS KLAUS AND MARLIES MÜHLBAUER TOOK OVER THE MANUFACTURE IN 2001. TODAY THE BRAND IS BACK ON COURSE, WITH REGULAR COLLECTIONS THAT COMBINE CONTEMPORARY DESIGN WITH TRADITIONAL MILLINERY TECHNIQUES.

In 2001 Klaus Mühlbauer took over the businesses from his parents.

Mühlbauer Hutmanufaktur is a millinery workshop based near Schwedenplatz in Vienna. Founded in 1903 by Julianna Mühlbauer together with her husband Robert in the Viennese suburb of Floridsdorf, the company grew quickly and, led by Julianna's son, went on to open 16 stores around Vienna. Now run by the fourth generation, siblings Klaus and Marlies are steering the venerable hatmaker back to its roots by focusing on hand-finished headwear of the highest quality. Mühlbauer hats can be found worldwide in some of the world's most renowned retail destinations including Le Bon Marché in Paris, 10 Corso Como in Milan, Isetan in Tokyo, and Harrods in London.

Mülbauer's fortunes suffered in the 1960s when styles changed and the demand for hats decreased dramatically. When Klaus and Marlies took over the business in 2001, the company's heritage had largely been forgotten. With the brand having turned its focus primarily to women's clothes in the interim, Klaus and Marlies returned the attention to headwear, shutting down all but two of the stores around Vienna, transforming one into a hat boutique, and taking production cues from high-end fashion houses with bi annual collections shown globally and lookbooks created in collaboration with famous artists and designers.

Some of Mühlbauer's hats are sewn from patterns like clothes, but the majority are made from felt or straw, shaped and stretched on a wooden mold. The process for a felt hat starts with a fur felt cone. To make the hat stable and weather resistant, the cone is soaked in a stiffening starch-based solution and then wrung out. The damp felt cone is then steamed under a bell in order to become stretchable and easier to mold. Afterwards it's removed from the steaming

left: In order to shape a hat, the damp felt cone is steamed under a bell so it becomes stretchable and moldable. It is then removed from the steaming bell and stretched while still hot.

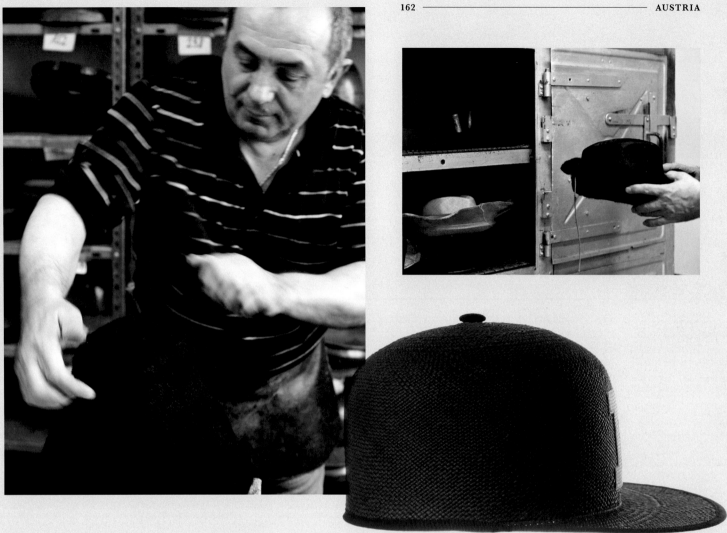

bell and stretched while still hot, with the felt hood then being fixed on to a wooden block, and dried in a special oven at 70°C for two to three hours. When it comes out, the hat is finished in its raw state, at which point it's sent off for finishing where the surface treatment of the shaped hat is applied. With great care, the hat is brushed, ironed, steamed, and dried, and the blocked and sanded hat now moves on to the millinery department where it receives its final polish. The trimmers decorate the hat with ribbons, buttons, buckles or feathers relevant to the design concept and, finally, the material surpluses are removed; the inner band and Mühlbauer label are sewn on as the finishing touch. Klaus feels his biggest reward from combining traditional craftsmanship and modern design are the hats they produce, "The result of my work itself: the hat. I have an idea, I draw it on paper, I think of materials, colors, trimmings, I put it into production, I change things and put in production again, I might change things again, and then some moments later I hold the hat in my hands, try it on me or others and if it looks good and fits well, I am happy and feel rewarded."

KLAUS FEELS HIS BIGGEST REWARD COMBINING TRADITIONAL CRAFTSMANSHIP AND MODERN DESIGN ARE THE HATS THEY PRODUCE!

Today, the atelier employs 16 people and produces nearly 13,000 headpieces per year, all handmade in its 1000-square-foot facility. Over the years, the company has designed and produced hundreds of molds, with the prototypes being made in-house from a mix of wood shavings and adhesive. The more durable molds come from a manufacturer in the Czech Republic and each mold is labeled with its unique shape and number. Mühlbauer has around 5000 different shapes, and most of the hats are made from the finest rabbit fur from Portugal, with the straw hats hailing from Ecuador and Panama. •

DANIEL HEER
MATTRESS MAKER

THE SCION OF A FAMILY FROM LUCERNE WHO HAVE BEEN MAKING HORSEHAIR MATTRESSES SINCE 1907, DANIEL HEER FIRST SET OUT ON A DIFFERENT PATH BEFORE DISCOVERING THAT HE COULD CONTINUE THE FAMILY'S CRAFTING TRADITIONS ON HIS OWN TERMS.

The Heer name has been synonymous with leather saddles and *Rosshaarmatrazen,* or traditional horsehair mattresses, since 1907 when Benedikt Heer founded his workshop in Lucerne, Switzerland. Known for its durability and comfort, horsehair has long been considered a staple of high-quality upholstery, but its use has declined in recent times owing to the introduction of cheaper synthetic materials. After training as an apprentice with his family, Daniel Heer, Benedikt's great-grandson, moved to Berlin, and wondered for a while whether his days in the Rosshaarmatrazen trade were over. As is often the way with family businesses, the distance allowed him to reflect on his heritage, and when he finally decided to return to the craft, it was to be on his own terms.

Today he handcrafts mattresses and leather goods at Manufaktur Heer, his workshop in Mitte, Berlin. Horsehair is ordered in bales from Toggenburger & Co., the only spinnery of its kind in Switzerland, which also supplies the white horsetail hair for the mattresses of the royal families of Sweden and England. Hair from the mane gives a medium firmness, while the tail hair is much firmer, and the customer's preference is taken into account before Daniel begins work on each piece. It requires the hair from more than 40 horses to create each mattress, a material particularly well suited to the task, owing to its elasticity, high tensile strength, and ability to absorb moisture. It also eliminates odors, acts well to conserve heat, and is of course a totally natural and sustainable product.

IT REQUIRES THE HAIR FROM MORE THAN 40 HORSES TO CREATE EACH MATTRESS, A MATERIAL PARTICULARLY WELL SUITED TO THE TASK, OWING TO ITS ELASTICITY, HIGH TENSILE STRENGTH AND ABILITY TO ABSORB MOISTURE.

To create each mattress, Heer carefully sculpts around 33 pounds of horsehair into three layers, two feet high. He's keen to emphasize the fact that the mattresses themselves are "built, not stuffed." Knowing instinctively when the mattress has reached the correct firmness and density, the horsehair is then covered in virgin fleece before being dressed in fabric (his preference is for Kvadrat wool) and the edges rolled to give the mattress its form. Expert needlework is used to refine the shape, with more

Swiss designer Daniel Heer in his Berlin workshop.

TO CREATE EACH MATTRESS, HEER CAREFULLY SCULPTS AROUND 33 POUNDS OF HORSE-HAIR INTO THREE LAYERS, TWO FEET HIGH.

above: In collaboration with Thomas van Asseldonk, Daniel Heer uses the "wedge" method to combine wood and leather without glue or nails.

right: Daniel Heer constructs each horsehair mattress following his customers' wishes and according to the Heer family tradition.

The collections of handmade bags are manufactured with traditional leather craftsmanship methods.

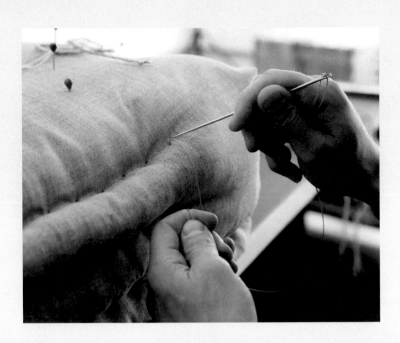

The craft of making Rosshaar-matratzen, horsehair mattresses, has been in Swiss artisan Daniel Heer's family since 1907, when his great-grandfather Benedikt Heer opened a saddlery in Lucerne, Switzerland.

than 1000 individual stitches required for a mattress measuring 1x2 meters. Finally, tufted buttons are created from the same fabric, holding the horsehair interior in place inside the mattress. Such is the expert construction of the Rosshaarmatrazen, and the quality of the materials used that they will easily last a lifetime and can be passed on to future generations. Each piece is crafted entirely by Daniel, and the only maintenance required is a refurbishment every 15 years, and an annual "sun bath" to allow the natural material to aerate.

The weight of expectation that you will continue in the family trade can be a heavy burden, and it was important to Daniel that when he did take up the mantle, he could use his accumulated knowledge to realize his own vision. Alongside the mattresses, each of which takes him two days to make, he has created a collection of leather goods inspired by the saddlemaker's craft.

With clean, architectural forms and visible stitching, again entirely made by hand, the lineage of the saddler is clearly visible. More recently, he collaborated with carpenter Thomas van Asseldonk to create a small collection of furniture combining traditional carpentry techniques with his horsehair mattresses. Retaining the same honest but refined aesthetic, his furniture places an emphasis on simplicity, function and, naturally, durability. Named "Keil" after the German word for a wedge, also used in a technique for seamlessly joining wooden sections without the need for wood or nails, the pieces also recall classic upholstery methods, with woven leather meshwork left visible rather than concealed under fabric. For Daniel's AM-PM daybed, he references the almost forgotten concept of temporary rest; fitting, perhaps, that someone on this unique journey has found even more ways to reference the past in a thoroughly modern way. •

ELISA STROZYK
INDUSTRIAL DESIGNER

TOYING WITH THE NOTIONS OF FORM AND FUNCTION, INDUSTRIAL DESIGNER ELIZA STROZYK HAS COLLABORATED WITH GERMAN FURNITURE MAKER BÖWER ON A WOODEN TEXTILE CONCEPT THAT BLURS THE LINE BETWEEN MATERIALS AND THEIR TRADITIONAL USES.

German bespoke interiors and furniture company Böwer was founded as a small local carpentry workshop in Neuenkirchen, north-west Germany in 1888 and has become known for its outstanding furniture that is serially manufactured and often designed in collaboration with young furniture designers. Today, run by siblings Anja and Stefan Böwer, the architect and interior designer team, their collection draws on generations of knowledge and experiences ranging from their customized interior projects to extensive designer collaborations. Promoting craft and precision, translated into a modern collection that is characterized by elaborate details with a subtle use of color, their work now also serves as the foundation for the development of their new line of furniture.

Continuing the company's tradition of fostering dialogue with a selection of internationally acclaimed designers like Werner Aisslinger, Eric Degenhardt, Konstantin Grcic, Sebastian Herkner, and Cecilie Manz, Böwer has launched a collection of wooden carpets with textile designer Elisa Strozyk. Strozyk studied Textile and Surface Design at the Kunsthochschule in Berlin and went on to study for an MA in Future Textiles at London's Central Saint Martins. Her work pushes the boundaries of perception between two and three dimensions, often traversing the frontiers between categories and materials. Before collaborating with Böwer, she received the German Design Award and the Salone del Mobile Satellite Award.

The striking wooden carpet is one of the products from their ongoing project titled Wooden Textiles. The project is the result of Strozyk researching the possibility of imbuing wood with textile properties and experimenting with methods of making the material flexible and soft. The outcome is a creation that can be rolled up and scrunched, but is also flat and smooth. It is half-wood, half-textile, and sits between hard and soft, challenging what can be expected from the materials used. Made from three-ply veneer, oak, mahogany, walnut, and linen, carrying names such as Ashdown, Mortimer, Sherwood, and Wentwood, the extraordinary pieces are built of geometric components that can be shaped into a structure. As a moldable sculpture or an innovative and distinctive floor accent, the wooden carpet is an expression of futuristic textile design in its most experimental form. "It looks and smells familiar but feels strange, as it is able to move and shape in unexpected ways," Elisa explains. "The wooden carpet is a three-dimensional carpet made from wood. Also being something you would not expect from a carpet: a room object that cannot be defined. The wooden carpet blurs the boundaries between a common carpet

Designer Elisa Strozyk working on her piece Wooden Textiles.

PROMOTING CRAFT AND
PRECISION, TRANSLATED
INTO A MODERN COLLECTION
THAT IS CHARACTERIZED
BY ELABORATE DETAILS WITH
A SUBTLE USE OF COLOR.

Elisa Strozyk is researching ways
to provide wood with textile properties
by testing methods that turn
it into a flexible and soft material.

and traditional wood flooring. It's a decorative product to play with. It can be shaped to form a multifaceted and exciting object, or you arrange it flat on the floor."

In order to realize this unique material, that can also be used as curtains, drapes, and upholstery, Strozyk and Böwer had to design and deconstruct a flexible wooden surface into separate pieces that were then attached to a textile base. The wood is cut by laser, and each one of the tiles are attached to the textile base by hand to compose the surface and create the best

possible fit. The Ashdown carpet, which is the simpler construction, is made of a mix of linen, oak, maple, and beech whereas the more complicated constructions like the Westwood are made up of cherry, pear, mahogany, and bubinga woods. By collaborating with young designers, Böwer is keeping itself at the forefront of contemporary European design, as well as providing these designers with the opportunity to explore the almost limitless potential of working with wood. •

above: Each wooden carpet is made up of rows of triangular shapes that are dyed to form various geometric patterns.

right: The lights and cabinets of the "Accordion" collection are the result of a collaboration between designer Elisa Strozyk and artist Sebastian Neeb.

JUNIPER RIDGE
WILD DISTILLERY

HALL NEWBEGIN AND HIS TEAM AT JUNIPER RIDGE HAVE CREATED THE WORLD'S ONLY WILD FRAGRANCE DISTILLERY, VENTURING INTO THE MOUNTAINS, FORESTS, AND LAKES OF NORTH AMERICA TO DISTILL THEIR PERFUMES AND ESSENTIAL OILS.

The world's only "wild fragrance company," Juniper Ridge is the closest thing you can find to a mountain in a bottle, producing fragrances, soap, and incense evoking the scents of the wild nature of the west coast of America. Based in the Pacific Northwest and describing themselves as outlaws in the industry, designer Hall Newbegin and his colleagues Obi Kaufmann and Tom Accettola hike together the backcountry to bring natural, organic smells back to the city. He says, "I think we're sometimes seen as the perfume world's weirdo, tree-hugging cousins, but in some ways we're even more traditional than the big perfume houses because we don't use synthetics. We've gone back to the old fragrance extraction techniques that were the only way perfume was made a hundred years ago—steam distillation, tincturing, and effleurage—the old ways to coax oils out of real plants and flowers that go back to Roman times. No one does this stuff anymore."

Hall thinks of himself as being an accidental perfumer and entrepreneur, inspired by the days of his youth, hiking and backpacking around the lakes and peaks of the Cascades Range and in Portland, Oregon as well as the smells of mountains, plants, and the wet earth. Admitting that the process can look pretty ridiculous at times, they can often be found crawling around on the ground, sniffing, touching, and collecting plants, flowers, trees, wild herbs, and moss in order to find the right tonalities and scents. The sample distillations take place on the road in the back of the company van, a converted whiskey still,

and are then formulated around the campfire in the evening. "Conversations on a trip might go something like, 'Wow, I wish we had an extraction of these lovely smelling Ponderosa Pine needles' or 'Hey, let's make an effleurage of these stream orchids,'" Hall says. Their products carry names such as Death Valley campfire incense, Cascade Glacier cabin spray and Winter Redwood solid perfume evoking the names of the places they were conceived, discovered, and created.

"We know we've gotten it right when we discover the right combination of ingredients transport us to the glacier country of Mt. Hood or a campfire in the Mojave Desert," Hall says. "We want our colognes to do more than just smell great—we want them to take you to the wild places that inspired them. Our muse is the quiet stillness of the mountains, the deep beauty of a place. When you wear a wildcrafted fragrance, you know it. It's like a little snapshot of the place it came from. The sunshine, the snow-melt, the forest breezes—they're all in there, the layers are incredible. If I can put a summer's day on Mt. Hood's timberline trail when the wildflowers are peaking into a bottle, well, that's just the most beautiful thing that there is or ever could be." As nature is ever changing, so is its smell. Because local conditions and foliage differ from season to season, each bottle is labelled with a harvest code, meaning that each fragrance batch from a particular area is unique. Answering an increasing demand for personalized and organic fragrances that go beyond the established perfume house staples, Juniper Ridge is out there in a whole new way. •

Distilling on the road.

"WHEN YOU WEAR A WILDCRAFTED
FRAGRANCE, YOU KNOW IT.
IT'S LIKE A LITTLE SNAPSHOT OF
THE PLACE IT CAME FROM."

right: In the pot, foraged ingredients are mixed together with some cold water. More water is then added to the pump, which is rigged to the pot by copper pipes that help condense the steam. A fire is lit, the pump is turned on, and the result is a wildcrafted scent.

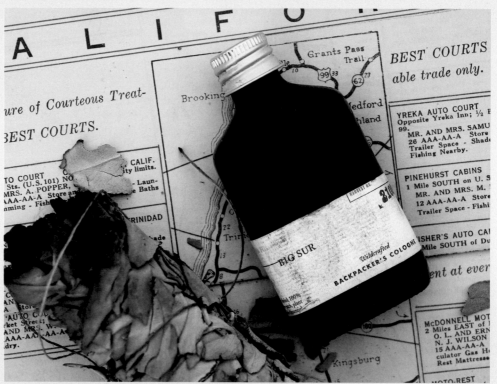

WEDNESDAY PAPER WORKS STATIONERS

SISTERS CHRISH AND JENNY KLOSE FOUNDED WEDNESDAY PAPER WORKS WITH A VIEW TO CREATING BEAUTIFUL, FUNCTIONAL STATIONERY PRODUCTS THAT STAND THE TEST OF TIME AND EMPLOY SUSTAINABLE PRODUCTION METHODS.

On a sunny Wednesday in 2011, sisters Chrish and Jenny Klose had the idea of founding paper company Wednesday Paper Works out of Kreuzberg in Berlin. Offering a variety of stationery products, the sisters found their calling by bridging the old with the new, and combining the best of bookbinding traditions with contemporary graphic elements.

A master bookbinder, Jenny, is the "hands" of the pair, turning her attention to the quality of the materials and tactile elements of the products, choosing papers and the binding techniques for each item they produce. She is fastidious in choosing materials that suit the character of each product, adding not only an aesthetic appeal but also fitness for purpose. An example of this thought process is when she spent time researching until she found a wipeable linen cloth, perfect to cover one of their cookbooks and withstand the stains it would encounter. Chrish, a graphic designer, is the "eyes" of the company, combining such diverse design elements as Jugendstil embossing and a passion for 1950s typography with

more striking modern elements so that old expressive styles and shapes are reinvigorated in a way that is timeless and warm. "We are two sisters with two different skills: master bookbinder and graphic designer. We always wanted to work together and it came very naturally to merge our talents," they say. "We are both deeply in love with paper and books, and love the feel and tactility of the materials we work with. Our different backgrounds allow us to create an exciting environment for new things to happen. Bookbinding is an old craft that only through merging with something new and modern can survive these exhilarating times."

The focus, however, is always on the paper. As a natural product that derives from the great woods of the world, the sisters are determined in their quest to make their product as sustainable as possible and have adopted the Charter for Sustainable Design as initiated by the Alliance of German Designers. The charter's key points cover topics from the regulation of pollutants, using energy-efficient processes,

Founders of Wednesday Paper Works, Jenny and Chrish Klose.

"WE BELIEVE THAT PAPER—
AS A MEDIUM—HAS THE POWER
AND QUALITY TO GET YOU
CONNECTED AGAIN."

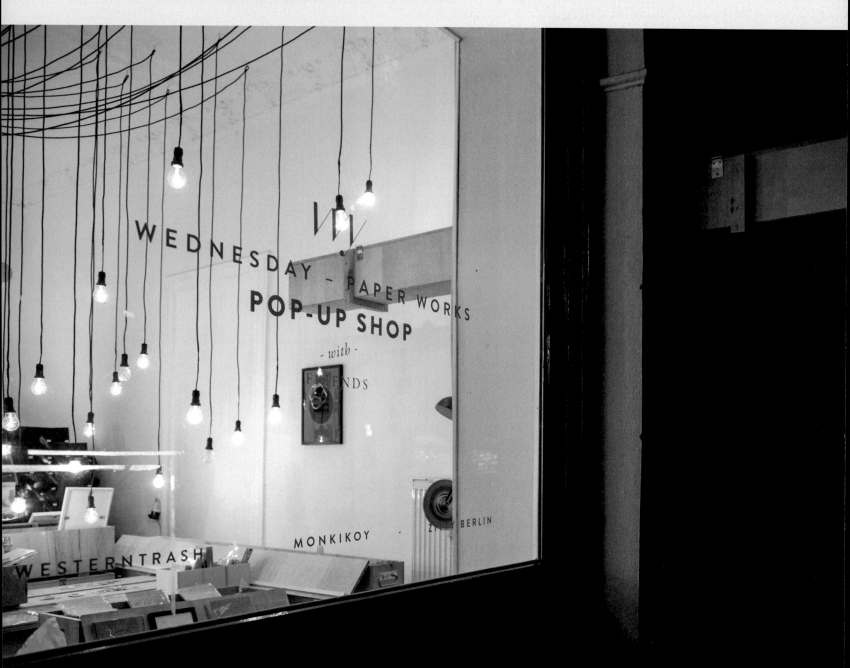

above: Papermaking tools: embossing
machines and a book press.

right: Lilo writing pad and
Eno notebook.

creating long-lasting products and social responsibility which provide the customer with a deeper sense of enjoyment and pleasure as they will know that by purchasing a Wednesday Paper Works product they are contributing to a better, less wasteful world. "We believe that in our stressful modern times, we need to get back to basics. We believe that paper—as a medium—has the power and quality to get you connected again," they add. "Our products are created from our own needs and interests, and reflect modern life that is found someplace between work, computer, leisure, and finding inspiration."

The Baby Journal, their most successful release to date, originally came about as Chrish was looking for an album in order to document the first year of her son's life but found nothing that she felt corresponded to her own vision in terms of quality, design, sustainability, and innovation. Cleverly, the journal can be

expanded as the baby grows and personalized for each child with its name, creating an object that combines all aspects of their ethos into one—promoting the

"OUR PRODUCTS ARE CREATED FROM OUR OWN NEEDS AND INTERESTS, AND REFLECT MODERN LIFE THAT IS FOUND SOMEPLACE BETWEEN WORK, COMPUTER, LEISURE, AND FINDING INSPIRATION."

idea that paper encourages attentiveness and consideration, with slowness as a counterbalance to everything virtual, screen-based, or instant. It's at the meeting point of analog and touch where one finds true authenticity. •

right: Jenny embossing the
cover of the recipe journal.

STÄHLEMÜHLE
DISTILLERY

A FORMER BOOK PUBLISHER, CHRISTOPH KELLER

BOUGHT AN ABANDONED MILL COMPLEX

IN SOUTHERN GERMANY AND TRANSFORMED

IT INTO AN AWARD-WINNING DISTILLERY

SPECIALIZING IN GINS, EAUX DE VIE, AND

HERB BRANDIES MADE USING RARE NATURAL

INGREDIENTS, EITHER SOURCED LOCALLY

OR GROWN ON SITE.

Originally an art book publisher, Christoph Keller founded the Stählemühle distillery in Eigeltingen, southern Germany on the site of a former mill in 2010. Enlisting the help of architect Philipp Mainzer to transform the existing structures, they created a distillery and tasting suite with an emphasis on traditional materials used in a contemporary context. The space forms a suitably striking background to the remarkable work of the distillery, which specializes in fruit schnaps, eaux-de-vie, and herb brandies, as well as two gins, Monkey 47 and Schwarzwald Dry Gin. Through these varied spirits, Christoph sought to explore the tastes of nature itself. He wanted to celebrate the fact that our formative sensorial memories make a hugely significant contribution to the way we experience flavors and aromas. "When people taste one of our spirits, they might say 'this tastes like the plums I had in my childhood'," says Christoph. "And we tell them this plum is still there!"

Although he came to distilling with no prior knowledge or experience, he has since gone on to win numerous awards for his spirits both in Germany and internationally, and the Stählemühle distillery is now considered to be one of the top ten distilleries in the world. While the technical and artistic skills required in distilling obviously differ significantly from those of a publisher, Christoph notes that he brought with him a sense of curiosity and a willingness to experiment. Interestingly, he adds that alongside Stählemühle, almost half of the world's top ten distillers were new to the craft when they started, which has allowed them to approach it with fresh eyes and an adventurous resolve.

Today he produces around 200 spirit varieties in small batches from a phenomenal list of fruits and natural botanical ingredients including wild plums, rowan berries, and medlars which are either grown on site, foraged, or bought in from the local area. Using a process of maceration, distillation, and percolation, unique mixtures of botanicals are steeped in a mash before being distilled in beautiful copper stills. As the mash mixture is heated, evaporation

Christoph Keller, master distiller.

above: Stählemühle spirits mature
for a period of four months up
to four years. This maturing cellar
was planned and designed
by e15 designer Philipp Mainzer.

right: Eau de Vie glasses by Austrian
glassmakers J. & L. Lobmeyer.

"WHEN PEOPLE TASTE ONE OF OUR
SPIRITS, THEY MIGHT SAY:
THIS TASTES LIKE A PLUM THAT
I HAD IN MY CHILDHOOD."

right: The distillery was custom-
made in 2010 by distillation
equipment manufacturer Markdorfer
Kupferschmiede Arnold Holstein.

begins and steam is created. As it is being produced, the steam is channeled through a mixture of fresh botanicals, which adds further complex flavor notes, before the steam is cooled back into a liquid and the spirit is collected at the other end. The resulting liquid, which has a very high alcohol content at this point, is then allowed to rest and "ripen" for a period of a few months to four years, during which time the molecules that are broken apart during the distillation process can reform, helping complex flavors to develop. The "ripened" spirits are finally married with very soft water from the Black Forest, which brings down the alcohol content to around 42%, and at last the spirits are ready to drink.

Christoph views the world of distillation as a melding of tradition, alchemy, and craftsmanship, and what he has managed to achieve with Stählemühle in the short time he has been working as a distiller is nothing short of astonishing. The site of the

"WE ARE WORKING IN THE SAME WAY DISTILLERS WORKED THREE CENTURIES AGO."

mill estate also includes a small plot of land where Christoph grows many of the raw materials used in his spirits and liqueurs. A particular passion is the nurturing and use of semi-extinct plant varietals in his distillation, as well as the promotion of organic farming practices. The distillery makes use of natural materials only, with no synthetic fruit extracts or even sugar used in the distillation process, but Christoph is keen to point out that this doesn't mean they aren't looking to the future. "We are working in the same way distillers worked three centuries ago," he says. "But we are also very research based. We experiment a lot, we do a lot of scientific research so that our production is kind of state of the art." •

right: Stählemühle Tasting Kit
No. 01 with 35 spirits.

BOCA DO LOBO
FURNITURE
MANUFACTURE

AT ONCE CLASSICAL AND THOROUGHLY MODERN, IN THE SPACE OF A FEW SHORT YEARS, HANDCRAFTED PORTUGUESE FURNITURE MAKERS BOCA DO LOBO HAVE CREATED AN AESTHETIC THAT IS ENTIRELY THEIR OWN.

Boca do Lobo is a multidisciplinary design practice and furniture brand, founded in 2005 by Amândio Pereira and Ricardo Magalhães in Oporto, Portugal. The emphasis of their work is on striking contemporary furniture created using the best in traditional Portuguese craftsmanship from their workshop in Rio Tinto on the outskirts of the city. A significant presence on the international design circuit, Boca do Lobo operates in more than 50 countries, and regularly shows at Maison & Objet in Paris, Decorex in London, and the Salone del Mobile in Milan. "Our founding principle is Emotional Design," says Patrícia Pinho. "Which means that every day we create exclusive design pieces meant to be deep emotional experiences."

The studio produces a wide range of distinctive furniture, including cabinets, consoles, seating, and lighting, selling to both the design industry and to private clients. In the short time since it opened for business, Boca do Lobo has created an aesthetic that draws from a range of references to create something entirely new. A combination of eccentric and unashamedly glamorous shapes, coupled with de luxe materials and world-class craftsmanship has proven

to be a winning formula. Touching on influences as diverse as high baroque, art deco, Victoriana, natural forms, and even the digital world, the designs inspire a kind of childlike wonder that requires the viewer to get up close and take a second look. Today, the brand is run by designer Marco Costa with a team of young, passionate designers and a team of skillful master artisans working together in harmony. "We believe we can show the world that tradition is never out of fashion. Boca do Lobo is, nowadays, one of the top furniture brands in the world and we achieved this status with our traditional roots and young talent."

Boca do Lobo's furniture is produced in its own factory outside Oporto, with more than 80 people currently employed there. They emphasize that the passion of their workers should be felt in the finished work. Casting, gilding, lacquer, filigree work, hand-carved wood, and hand-painted tiles all feature prominently, coming together in a seamless and refreshing way. "The north of Portugal, where the brand is based, is very rich when it comes to the skills we look for," she adds. "Generations of craftsmen with a level of perfection rarely seen anywhere else in the

London's Soho neighborhood was the inspiration behind one of Boca do Lobo's collections, the "Soho Sideboard." The collection was responsible for putting the brand on the international radar.

Boca do Lobo's design director
Marco Costa.

right clockwise: Royal dining table,
Forest cabinet, Monochrome console,
and Mondrian cupboard.

BOCA DO LOBO HAS CREATED
AN AESTHETIC THAT
DRAWS FROM A RANGE OF
REFERENCES, BUT MANAGES
TO BE ENTIRELY ITS OWN.

left: Boca do Lobo's Guggenheim
is handcrafted in Portugal
by master artisans according to
traditional methods.

"BOCA DO LOBO IS, NOWADAYS, ONE OF THE TOP FURNITURE BRANDS IN THE WORLD AND WE ACHIEVED THIS STAGE WITH OUR TRADITIONAL ROOTS AND YOUNG TALENT."

world! As I've said before, we are reviving these almost forgotten treasures and we want to elevate them to the major design stages in the world."

Mastery of any one of these techniques would be notable in itself, but when several are used together in such a coherent way, the effect is even more impressive. The result is a startling array of jewel-like pieces that play with traditional motifs to create something thoroughly modern. "From the very beginning, we've been working with extremely talented artisans who live for their art," Patrícia says. "We strive to revive these forgotten techniques and hidden talents. Many of our workers come from a family of artisans, so they were born into this art and have been practicing it their whole lives, from their childhood games, playing in the shop with those wonderful raw materials while their parents and grandparents were creating the most enchanting pieces, to perfecting their art as a profession." •

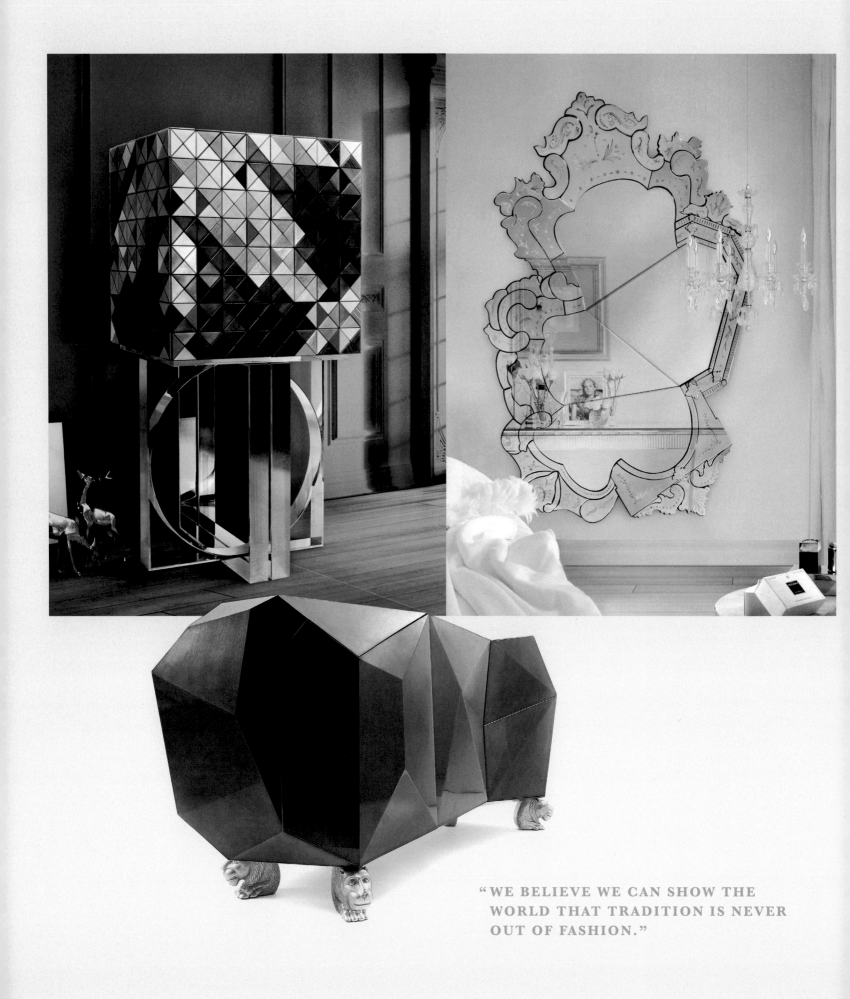

"WE BELIEVE WE CAN SHOW THE WORLD THAT TRADITION IS NEVER OUT OF FASHION."

LIVERANO & LIVERANO
TAILOR

ONE OF THE WORLD'S MOST RESPECTED NAMES IN BESPOKE

TAILORING, LIVERANO & LIVERANO EPITOMIZES THE

EFFORTLESS ELEGANCE OF CLASSIC FLORENTINE STYLE.

One of the last traditional tailors in Florence, and widely considered to be one of the best in the world, Liverano & Liverano is nothing less than an institution. The Liverano brothers, Antonio and Luigi, began as tailoring assistants in their native Puglia at a young age and, when he was old enough, Luigi moved to Florence to work with renowned tailor Commesatti. After two years, he set up his own atelier, and was soon joined by his brother Antonio who was only 11 years old at the time. This workshop would later come to be known as Liverano & Liverano when the brothers founded their first store on Via Panzani in 1960.

Today Antonio Liverano is still to be found at the cutting table six days a week, cutting out patterns for an ever-growing list of customers and overseeing his small team. With more than 70 years' experience, he is considered to be a world authority on men's tailoring. The Liverano house style is in the Florentine tradition (considered to fall somewhere between those other two bastions of gentlemen's style, Savile Row and Naples), with a soft, sloped shoulder, curved sleeve, generous lapel, and a tapered waist. The trousers are always pleated with a cuffed opening, giving an overall silhouette that is masculine while retaining an inherent elegance.

It's noteworthy that customers are not encouraged, as they are in some tailors, to bring their own fabric to be turned into a suit. The fabrics on offer at Liverano & Liverano are painstakingly chosen from British and Italian mills, and especially if it's your first suit there, Antonio will usually insist on choosing the fabric for you himself. It is often said that in bespoke tailoring, the tailor will make you the suit he wants to make, and this was never truer than at Liverano & Liverano. Questions of cut, fit, color, and style are all left to the Maestro.

The shop offers a fully bespoke service, whereby an entirely new pattern is created for each customer, and adapted over time as their body shape changes. It takes over 70 hours of meticulous handwork to create a two-piece suit, and usually two to three fittings are required to make adjustments during the process. A partnership with The Armoury, a men's outfitter based in Hong Kong, introduced the Liverano cut to an Asian audience, where it proved to be immensely popular. Antonio now makes several trips a year to the Far East to take the measurements of existing customers and introduce new clients to the brand, as well as running trunk shows in Korea, Japan, and the USA. •

Italian master tailor
Antonio Liverano.

WITH MORE THAN 70 YEARS'
EXPERIENCE, HE IS CONSIDERED
TO BE A WORLD AUTHORITY ON
MEN'S TAILORING.

MOYNAT
TRUNK MAKERS

ONCE AN ESTEEMED NAME IN FINE LUGGAGE MANUFACTURE, MOYNAT HAD DRIFTED INTO OBSCURITY BEFORE IT WAS RECENTLY BROUGHT BACK TO LIFE WITH AN INVESTMENT FROM BERNARD ARNAUD. TODAY THE HOUSE PRODUCES AN EXCEPTIONAL RANGE OF HANDMADE TRUNKS AND LEATHER GOODS FROM AN ATELIER IN PARIS.

Founded in 1849 by Pauline Moynat, notably the only woman trunk maker of the period, Moynat was a rarity in what at that time was very much a man's world. The house achieved great success in its early days, with several awards at the world's fair in Paris in the late 19th and early 20th centuries, but fell dormant in the 1970s. It was recently brought back to life through an investment from Bernard Arnaud. Ramesh Nair, formerly of Hermès, was appointed creative director and continues to work in this role today.

The house produces leather goods and luggage for men and women, with an emphasis on refined, understated design and superlative materials. For Ramesh, the product is about more than the final piece, it's the culmination of the steps that it takes to get there. From sourcing, cutting, stitching, and finishing the leather goods, it's the fact that Moynat products have to go through so many processes, all in the hands of a single craftsman, that makes them unique. There seems to be a quiet confidence in the quality of the work and a desire to allow the products to speak for themselves, with Ramesh keen to assert that in re-establishing Moynat, they were not trying to recreate the past, adding that heritage shouldn't be a ball and chain, but rather a springboard to jump off from and something to celebrate.

Moynat was an early innovator, with inventions like the first safe trunk for traveling with jewelry, the first bag named after a popular personality (spirited Belle Époque actress Rejane), and notably a trunk with a curved base allowing for transport on the roof of an automobile, which has become one of their signature designs today. Innovation is still a key tenet of the house's philosophy, down to tiny details like an extra eyelet for a strap next to the bag's handle to avoid two pieces of leather chafing aigainst each other and damaging the handle. A firm belief that innovation pushes craftsmanship forward and gives the maker an incentive to solve problems, alongside a desire to continually find new techniques are both fundamental principles that pervade everything Moynat does.

The fact that Moynat was founded by a pioneering woman continues to be relevant to the company today, in two of its essential codes: "curves and color." It was one of the first houses to offer trunks that were not only customizable by shape, but also by color. In the 19th century, natural pigments were used to develop the lacquer of the customer's choice, which was something fairly revolutionary in an era when the usual finishes would have been uniformly dark or monogrammed. A high degree of customization is another one of the signatures of the house

The iconic Réjane bag.

THE HOUSE PRODUCES
LEATHER GOODS AND LUGGAGE
FOR MEN AND WOMEN, WITH
AN EMPHASIS ON REFINED,
UNDERSTATED DESIGN AND
SUPERLATIVE MATERIALS.

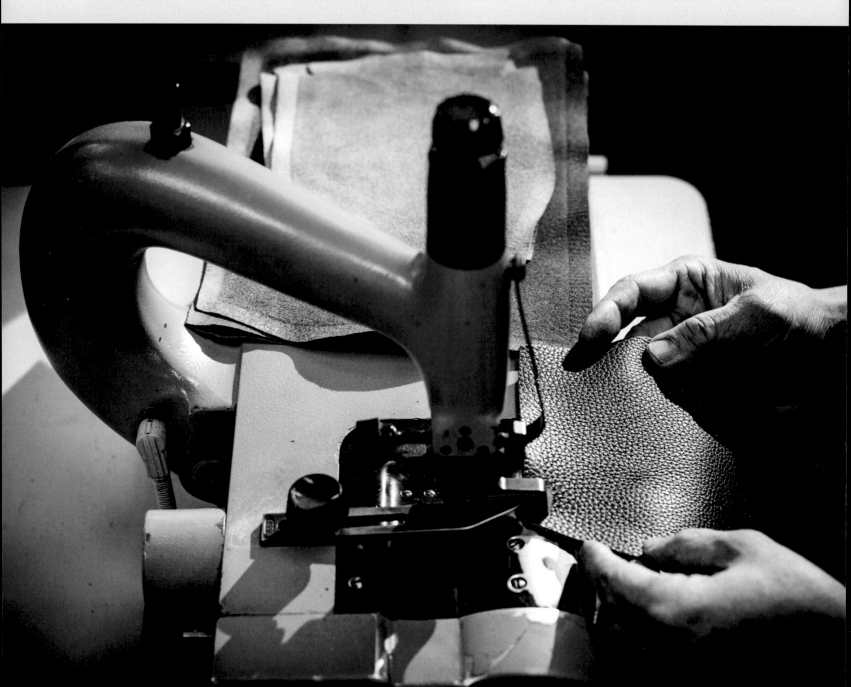

Moynat is the only French trunk manufactory whose atelier is located in the center of Paris.

that Ramesh and his team felt it was very important to champion in Moynat's modern iteration. The
challenge was to transfer this level of customization
from trunks (which would have been built to match
the shape and color of a specific car) to small leather
goods that can be used every day. Today, pieces can
be personalized with monogrammed initials in custom
typefaces or other motifs, each one painted by hand
and unique to the customer. Of course this all takes
a little time, but Ramesh is quick to point out that
any waiting list that builds up is simply a symptom
of working at full capacity, and that quality takes
time, rather than an attempt to foster an atmosphere
of artificial exclusivity.

For a leather brand working with such traditional
techniques, Ramesh's workforce is remarkably young.
He believes that the transmission of knowledge is not
only a necessity when dealing with very specialized,
often ancient ways of working, but also a responsibility to prevent these crafts from dying out. Each
individual piece, whether it is a trunk, a handbag or

a small leather item, is completely made from start to
finish by a single person. He estimates that around 50
percent of the time it takes to produce a piece is tak-
en up with the various stages of finishing, including
trimming, painting edges, and making handles. By
maintaining an atelier in the center of Paris, Ramesh
can have a direct and immediate influence on the design and manufacturing processes, something which
is essential to the way he works.

"For me and my team," Ramesh says, "Luxury
is about being able to exercise restraint, and at times
having to say no. It's about asking whether we need
to be in a certain product class just because a com-
petitor is." It's this attitude of making only as many
pieces as the workshop can comfortably handle, of
taking responsibility for the future of these crafts by
educating a young workforce, and the fact that they
have reached a level of quality in four years that has
taken some of their competitors more than 150 to
reach that really makes Moynat stand out. •

above: All products are 100%
made in France. Exotic leather is
entirely produced in Paris.
All the leathers and metallic parts
are sourced from French suppliers
to Moynat specifications.

FROM SOURCING, CUTTING,
STITCHING, AND FINISHING
THE LEATHER GOODS, IT'S THE
FACT THAT MOYNAT PRODUCTS
HAVE TO GO THROUGH SO MANY
PROCESSES, THAT MAKES
THEM UNIQUE.

BELLERBY & CO.
GLOBEMAKERS

UNABLE TO FIND THE PERFECT GLOBE AS A GIFT, PETER BELLERBY SET OUT ON A TWO-YEAR PERSONAL QUEST THAT BORDERED ON OBSESSION, EVENTUALLY LEADING TO HIM FOUNDING HIS OWN GLOBEMAKING COMPANY, BELLERBY & CO.

A search for a globe as a gift for his father's 80th birthday sparked a personal quest for Peter Bellerby, which led to him establishing his own globe making company in 2009. Driven by the poor quality of new globes available on the market, mostly those that were intended merely for reference rather than to inspire the viewer, he spent almost two years on the first globe as Bellerby & Co. Globemakers was born.

Peter's ambition when starting the company was to make the most "beautiful, original, and accurate globes ever made." This was coupled with the desire to promote the significance of handmade, limited edition products in our increasingly throw-away world. No mean feat perhaps, especially as he soon discovered that the master globemakers of the past had died without passing on their secrets. It never occurred to him when his journey began, that the reason no one was making globes today is because the process was so difficult.

The globes are cast as plaster-of-paris hemispheres created using resin molds and glued together to form a perfect sphere, with the margin for error at each stage being tiny. Counterbalance weights are placed inside before the halves are sealed to create a sphere, which allows the globes to spin smoothly

and come to a gentle, controlled halt. Next, the paper maps are applied in sections by hand. Because the paper is wet and is prone to moving as it dries, Peter estimates that teaching someone to make the smallest globe they produce takes a minimum of six months.

BELLERBY & CO. IS THE ONLY COMPANY WHICH HAS DEVELOPED A GLOBE THAT IS SUFFICIENTLY ROBUST AND DURABLE THAT IT CAN SIT ON ROLLER BEARINGS.

He found that the aging techniques already used on the market were primitive, and the cartography was often out of date or inaccurate. In fact, the first standard antique map they bought to work with shared the same inaccuracies as all pre-satellite maps, so he painstakingly spent time on Google Maps taking on the herculean task of poring over every inch of the globe to correct spelling errors and misplaced locations. Peter then stripped the map down to borders and place names, and replaced the existing text with a hand-drawn and historically accurate typeface. Meredith Owen, is Bellerby and Co.'s in-house artist,

Ballerby & Co. work together with specially-trained artists to help with the production and application of the maps in their London-based studio.

left: The sections of paper are
soaking wet when applied.
Even the slightest tension can
cause a rip, forcing the craftsman
to start again.

who has developed her own techniques for creating the transitions from land to sea, as well as for aging and varnishing the globes.

After visiting the National Maritime Museum archive, he found that most historic globes blacken over time due to the acidity of the glues used in the past. To combat this, Bellerby globes use a pH-neutral glue, and are coated in a UV protective varnish to ensure the colors stay true for hundreds of years to come. Bellerby & Co. is the only company which has developed a globe that is sufficiently robust and durable that it can sit on roller bearings, allowing it to be manually spun by the user in any direction. This creates a whole new way to interact with a globe, and coupled with their superlative accuracy and aesthetic beauty, it's not a surprise that of the three traditional globemakers currently in operation worldwide, Peter Barber, the head of the British Library map collection says that Bellerby & Co. are "the only ones worth talking about." They were asked to host the first ever exhibition of globes at the Royal Geographical Society, as well as collaborating with Martin Scorsese to create globes for his film *Hugo*.

All Bellerby Globes are made to order and in this way, each one is unique. Every process is undertaken in-house, and customers even have the option to add a geographical detail such as a mountain range named after themselves. It's remarkable to see such unwavering dedication to an almost forgotten craft, and to produce a product that not only flies above the competition, but that takes the offering into a whole new world. •

GULL LAKE BOAT WORKS
CANOE WORKSHOP

SPECIALIZING IN TRADITIONAL WOOD AND COMPOSITE BOAT CONSTRUCTION, MARC RUSSELL HAND-BUILDS CANOES AND KAYAKS WHICH CELEBRATE THE SPIRIT OF THE GREAT NORTH AMERICAN OUTDOORS.

Gull Lake Boat Works is a boat workshop that custom-builds wooden canoes, kayaks, and runabouts for discerning enthusiasts. Specializing in wood and composites, they build, repair, and restore all types of small watercraft on the shore of the lake that lends its name to the business in Ontario, Canada. It was founded out of necessity in 2008, by owner and head builder Marc Russell, when he was asked to repair and replace the aging fleet of antique cedar plank and canvas canoes at Kilcoo Camp, a venerable private summer camp for boys founded in 1932. Marc himself had attended the camp for almost twenty years, both as a camper and as a member of staff. Under an intensive apprenticeship with master builder Ron Frennette of Canadian Canoes, he was taught the craft and now combines traditional designs, modern methods, and meticulous handwork to create one-of-a-kind vessels including the Kilcoo 15'7" canoe, the modern equivalent of those found in the old fleet.

A small and personal operation, Marc describes the boats as being like children—some being terrible and temperamental to make, and some just coming together naturally. Primarily made out of wood, they all have a personality and an identity, the natural materials being what makes each boat so special, aiding their buoyancy and balance, and making them smoother to paddle.

Each boat requires 100 to 200 work hours to create. In addition to seventy board feet of white cedar wood from northern Ontario, white ash, 2,200 brass canoe tags from Massachusetts, brass stembands from Scandinavia, and impregnated and watertight canvas are used. The first step is to dress the rough cut cedar and chosen hardwood in the shop to exacting measurements before the hardwood elements are prepared: Stems are steam-bent and epoxy-laminated, inwales are steamed, and bent and both are attached to a solid mold. The cedar ribs are then soaked and steamed, making them supple and able to be bent around the mold and attached to the inwales and stems. To even out the rough edges, the ribs are then "faired"—sanded smooth to the desired profile before the cedar planking is nailed to the skeletal boat. The brass canoe tacks are driven through the plank and rib, hitting steel clinching bands and collapsing

Gull Lake Boat Works founder Marc Russell.

> **"ALL DESIGN HAS A TRACEABLE EVOLUTION, AND BOATS ARE NO DIFFERENT, SPECIFICALLY THE 'TRADITIONAL' NORTH AMERICAN CANOE."**

tightly upon themselves. At this stage, Mark carefully removes the hull from the mold, installing the decks, while checking that every tack, nail, and screw is tight as additional ribs and planks are attached.

After the joints and small gaps are filled with epoxy resin and filler, the hull is faired again and at this point receives two coats of spar varnish while the inner hull is checked for blemishes and prepared for varnishing. In total, each boat will receive up to eight coats. Then the canvas is stretched and carefully "gored," or cut to shape, and attached with brass tacks before being impregnated with another three to six layers of epoxy resin and fillers. Now, the hardwood

outwales, keel and brass stem bands are attached and all joints are sealed with epoxy resin while the trims, seats, thwarts, yokes, and lift handles are installed. Finally the canvas and epoxy are faired again, before the last detail, which is the anti-fouling undercoat, is applied, faired, and covered with up to ten coats of marine enamel in the desired color.

"All design has a traceable evolution, and boats are no different," says Marc. "Specifically, the 'traditional' North American canoe—from dug-out logs to birch bark or skin-on-frame, wood to aluminum to fiberglass, Royalex, Kevlar, and carbon fiber, the canoe has always been a willing subject and beneficiary for the growth of technological design and innovative use of combined materials. As such, the versatility, strength, and durability of composite construction in boatmaking has been apparent for centuries. Gull Lake Boat Works is furthering the practice by continuing to fuse the best of design, method, and material." •

right: Gull Lake Boat Works creates custom canoes and kayaks that are made to last for generations.

A SMALL AND PERSONAL
OPERATION, MARC DESCRIBES
THE BOATS AS BEING LIKE
CHILDREN—SOME BEING
TERRIBLE AND TEMPERAMENTAL
TO MAKE AND SOME JUST
COMING TOGETHER NATURALLY.

left: Each canoe takes 100
to 200 man-hours to execute.

above: Marc Russell planking
the ribs of a canoe hull.

NYMPHENBURG
PORCELAIN MANUFACTURE

LOCATED IN MUNICH'S NYMPHENBURG PALACE, THE ROYAL PORCELAIN MANUFACTURE HAS ESTABLISHED ITSELF FIRMLY AT THE PINNACLE OF TRADITIONAL GERMAN DECORATIVE ARTS.

Porzellan Manufaktur Nymphenburg, more commonly known as Royal Nymphenburg, is a handmade porcelain manufacturers established in 1753. Since 1761, it has been situated in the Nymphenburg Palace in Munich, the capital of Bavaria in Germany, and since 1975 the factory has been leased to the Wittelsbach Compensation Fund that is run by the Duke of Bavaria, a descendant of the Wittelsbach family that ruled Bavaria until 1918. The porcelain carries the family's diamond-shaped crest as its own.

The company's story begins with the accession of Maximilian II Joseph, the Prince-elector of Bavaria, when he commanded the establishment of a variety of manufacturing companies in the region in order to rescue the state's ailing finances. It was not until 1754 that the attempts at making porcelain were successful, and in that same year, the porcelain sculptor Franz Anton Bustelli came to work at the factory. The

following year it received its first commission from the Bavarian court and subsequently started painting its porcelain in colors, which paved the way for further patronages and orders, especially for dinner services with copies of famous paintings or Bavarian landscapes. By the mid-19th century the company had fallen on such bad times that privatization was necessary and all artistic production was halted. It was not until 1887, with Albert Bäuml and his family, that the factory returned to its roots with a more artistic outlook. Alongside historical copies of previous works by Bustelli, Dominikus Auliczek the Elder, and Johann Melchior, they also started putting out contemporary and elegant Jugendstil ceramics which were very much in fashion at that time.

Porcelain, once described by philosopher Arthur Schopenhauer as "frozen music," is made from the ground raw ingredients of kaolin or white china clay,

PLATES, BOWLS AND CUPS
ARE SHAPED ON WHEELS, WHILE
DETAILED FIGURINES OR
FIGURES ARE METICULOUSLY
CONSTRUCTED AND
DECORATED FOR UP TO A
MONTH FOR A VERY COMPLI-
CATED MODEL, WITH THE PAINT-
WORK TAKING UP TO A WEEK.

quartz, and feldspar. Purifying the components of this "white gold" paste is a challenging process, involving among other techniques, laying it down on the cool floor of the building's cellar and letting it mature like wine. During the heating stage of production, pieces spend 36 hours in ovens at 1400˚C, an environment that will make them shrink by around one sixth of their original size. The result is the pure white, particularly smooth, and hard finish for which Nymphenburg porcelain is known. Plates, bowls, and cups are shaped on wheels, while detailed figurines or figures are meticulously constructed and decorated for up to a month for a very complicated model, with the paintwork taking up to a week. For the more exclusive work with 24-carat gold ornamentation, the polishing of the metal on porcelain with agate tools can take three times as long. Each piece is marked

with the Nymphenburg stamp, and the modeler's and painter's signatures. Producing almost 20,000 pieces each year, the archives at Nymphenburg contain a model of every single piece that has ever been produced, and can be remade at the request of a client.

Managed in recent years by Baron Egbert von Maltzahn, Nymphenburg is an outstanding example of traditional practices kept alive over the centuries. The house has recently experienced a new wave of interest, buoyed by a focus on collaborations with young designers, keeping to the Nymphenburg ethos of championing artists of its time. Recently this has become even more pronounced with the matching of Bustelli's classic Commedia dell'Arte pieces with clothes from fashion designers including Christian Lacroix, Elie Saab, and Karl Lagerfeld. •

left: More than 30,000 shapes
are stored at the model and mold
archives.

above: For over 260 years,
thousands of pigments and oxides
for all the paints used in production
have been mixed and manufactured
in the in-house paint laboratory.

PRODUCING ALMOST 20,000 PIECES
EACH YEAR, THE ARCHIVES AT
NYMPHENBURG CONTAIN A MODEL
OF EVERY SINGLE PIECE
THAT HAS EVER BEEN PRODUCED.

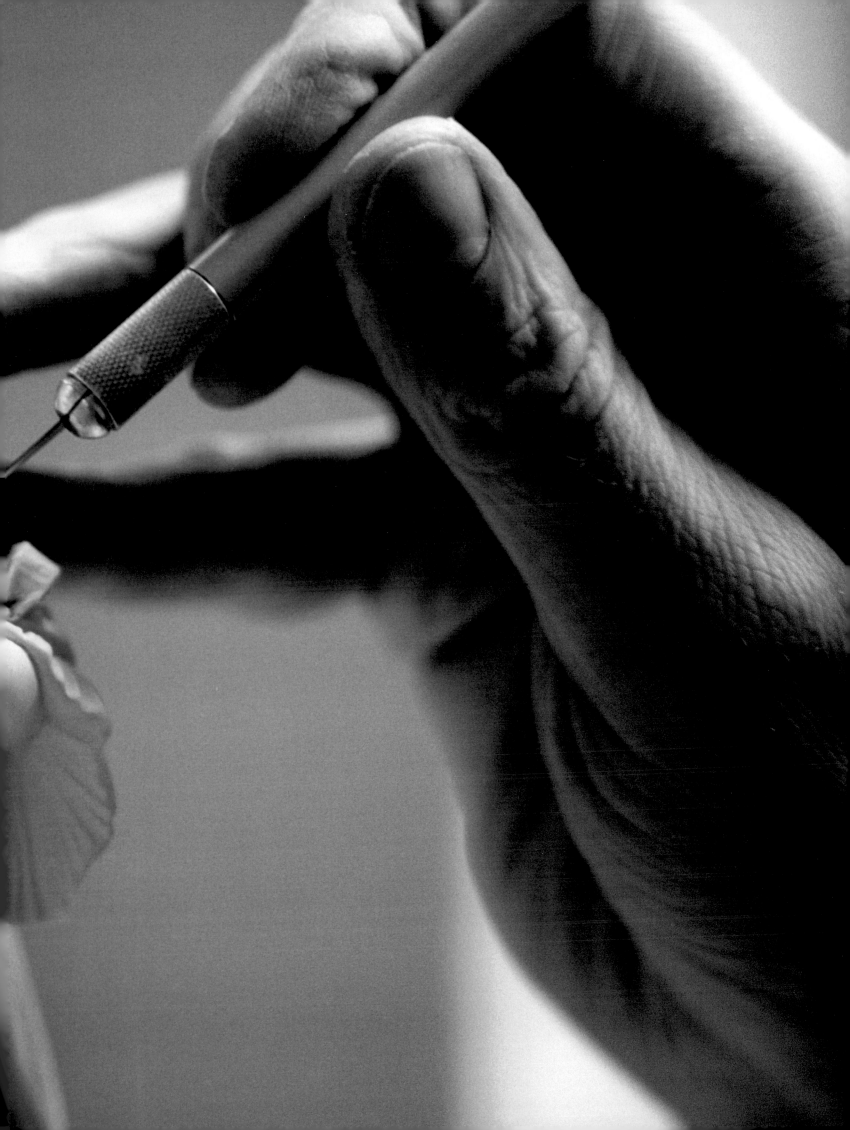

FLORENTINE KITCHEN KNIVES
KNIFE MAKERS

STARTING LIFE AS A PROJECT IN HIS FINAL YEAR OF COLLEGE AT THE SHENKAR SCHOOL OF ENGINEERING AND DESIGN IN TEL AVIV, FLORENTINE KITCHEN KNIVES IS A KNIFE RANGE FOUNDED BY TOMER BOTNER THAT BRINGS TRADITIONAL TECHNIQUES AND COLLABORATIVE EFFORT TO THE FORE.

Florentine Kitchen Knives began life as a final college project for Tomer Botner at the Shenkar School of Engineering and Design in Tel Aviv. He wanted to celebrate the highly skilled craftspeople at work in Florentin (Tomer added the 'e'), a bohemian neighborhood in a southwesterly corner of the city, more usually associated with the carpentry and upholstery trades. Following a successful crowdfunding campaign to create the first 100 knives made available to the public, he now produces the small range in limited, numbered batches in collaboration with a cutlery manufacture in the Portuguese village of Santa Catarina. The collection currently features a 200-mm chef's knife, a 235-mm bread knife, and sets of six 120-mm steak knives, created in partnership with Michelin three-star chef Sergio Herman from The Jane restaurant in Antwerp.

A collaborative spirit is at the heart of the Florentine Kitchen Knives ethos, with more than 17 suppliers, craftsmen, and professionals—from Florentin and internationally—involved with their production, from the physical elements like steel supply, through sharpeners, finishers, and leather craftsmen, to the branding, digital, and packaging components. "I hope my knives will help brand Florentin as a place of quality design and quality makers," he says. Having worked in the restaurant trade himself, both in and outside of the kitchen, it was very important to Tomer that the form followed the function of these tools, and that he created something that was as effective as it was aesthetically beautiful. To this end, he continues to work with various cooks, chefs, and other knife makers today to continually refine the design and optimize the shape for best handling and performance.

Shorter and wider than a traditional kitchen knife, the chef's knife has significant weight, and features a curved spine and blade more often seen in Asian-style knives. In the hands of a skilled operator, the blade shape allows for a rocking-style chopping motion, while the weight of the blade allows for precision cutting, with the knife itself doing most of the work.

A COLLABORATIVE SPIRIT IS AT THE HEART OF THE FLORENTINE KITCHEN KNIVES ETHOS, WITH MORE THAN 17 SUPPLIERS, CRAFTSMEN, AND PROFESSIONALS.

above: Founder of Florentine Kitchen Knives, Tomer Botner, aims to bring a spirit of craft and cooperation to local communities.

right: The blades are created with the help of 17 local suppliers, craftsmen, and professionals from Tel Aviv's Florentine neighborhood.

Each blade is individually numbered, reminding the user that they are produced in very limited runs, and imbuing each piece with more personality.

The knife handles employ a distinctive stacking technique, with various materials—many of which are sourced locally in Portugal—including steel, brass, colored polymers, oak, walnut, and stabilized leather—precision-cut to the correct disc size, using laser cutting, water jet or an electronic knife depending on the material. The discs are then stacked along the length of the handle in such a way that the blade is perfectly balanced in the hand and a unique stripe pattern is created. The discs are then secured in place by a brass bolster. Combining manual skills with technology, the stacking process is designed to allow each worker in the workshop to express their creativity while still ensuring that the finished products are of a consistent form, and meet the quality required.

The idea that global and local thinking needn't be mutually exclusive concepts is a refreshing one.

It is possible to promote the heritage and skills of an area, as well as encouraging a new generation of designers and makers to pick up their tools, while also looking further afield for the best expertise to suit each given situation. "I looked for the best place to manufacture for a long time and it was important to me to find a place with a cutlery heritage where I can learn, and in Portugal I have that," he says. "I would love to be helping this craft develop here but instead I'm helping it survive somewhere else, in a country which is having a tough time right now." Tomer plans to continue collaborating with the community he has built up around Florentine Kitchen Knives, with new product lines to come in the future. "We want to grow slowly and focus on quality," he adds. "We expand through collaborations, always collaborations. Everything on the table right now is a collaboration, which hopefully, will turn into a long-lasting relationship." •

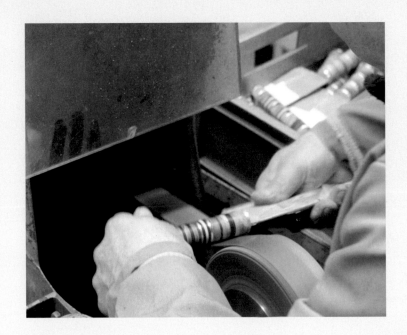

HOSOO
TEXTILE DESIGN

THE HOSOO FAMILY ARE ONE OF THE LONGEST UNBROKEN LINES OF TRADITIONAL WEAVERS IN JAPAN WITH A LINEAGE THAT CAN BE TRACED BACK TO SIXTH-CENTURY KYOTO. TODAY THEY CONTINUE THIS DISTINGUISHED TRADITION, AND LOOK TO THE FUTURE WITH CONTEMPORARY FASHION AND INTERIORS COLLABORATIONS.

Tracing their techniques back to the sixth century silk industry in Kyoto, the Hosoo family are one of the longest unbroken family lines of traditional weavers in Japan. They are renowned for their exceptional skill and traditional Japanese three-dimensional weaving method known as Nishijin, named after the city's textile district. Originally used for kimonos and obi sashes, the Nishijin fabrics became so popular amongst the high-ranking monks, the distinguished samurai class, and the Imperial courts of Kyoto that the family founded a company to meet the growing demand in 1688.

Still based in their original premises, Hosoo creates Nishijin fabrics that for centuries have been recognized for their intricacy, detail, and beauty. Nishijin are diagonally woven fabrics created by using many different colored yarns and weaving them together in decorative designs, which range from dual to multi-tone and from subtle to very vibrant colors. The first step is to decide on the pattern of the fabric. In the past these patterns would often have been floral or inspired by Japanese folklore, but can now

be designed according to a particular client's wishes. Before the weaving starts, the yarns are dyed with meticulous care in order to imbue the color scheme of each design with a rich, deep tone. After the yarns have been dyed, the silk is fitted onto yarn frames for easier handling during the warping and weaving stages of the process. Unique for Nishijin is the next step, the application of gold and silver washi paper shreds that are created by pasting the metals onto washi papers, then weaving them on with silk thread, which gives the fabric more strength and durability. For the weaving, the heddle is the focal part of the loom, since each thread in the warp passes through it, and separates the warp threads for the passage of the weft. Each heddle has an eye in the center through which the warp is threaded, creating an intense and multidimensional fabric

In 2011, during the economic downturn in Japan, Masataka Hosoo, the 12th generation of the Hosoo family, realized that the company's future rested on building an international presence. Looking to establish recognition outside of Japan, he partnered

Once a Hosoo pattern has been developed, a color-schemed digital template is created and used as the blueprint for textile production.

HOSOO CREATES NISHIJIN FAB-
RICS THAT FOR CENTURIES HAVE
BEEN RECOGNIZED FOR THEIR
INTRICACY, DETAIL, AND BEAUTY.

right: Collage fabric designed
by OeO Design Studio on a bespoke
desk at the Wallpaper Handmade
exhibition during the Salone del
Mobile in Milan in 2013.

with Danish design studio OeO with the objective of offering their textiles to the high-end fashion and contemporary design industries. Developing the communication platform, establishing strategic partnerships, and developing and designing a wide range of new textile designs and products, the partnership, with OeO has been a successful one. In four years, the company has provided finely crafted custom fabrics to designers and architects all over the world, gracing interiors by Peter Marino for Christian Dior, Chanel, and Louis Vuitton as well as the runways of Thom Browne and Mihara Yasuhiro.

Masataka comments: "Hosoo pushes the boundaries of textiles by combining the qualities of traditional craftsmanship with highly developed skills within three-dimensional weaving. These unique weaving techniques add depth, structure, and detail to the textile in the actual weaving process besides creating the pattern. In addition, Hosoo textiles are crafted using only the best Kyoto yarns dyed with meticulous care to compose individually toned color schemes. The result is an exceptional, rich texture and distinct tactile experience. Traditionally crafted, yet new and intriguing." The successful refocusing of the company has also led to the opening of a shop, Hosoo Kyoto, where the diverse applications of the fabrics are displayed in homeware, accessories and furniture. •

HOSOO PUSHES THE BOUNDARIES OF TEXTILES BY COMBINING THE QUALITIES OF TRADITIONAL CRAFTSMANSHIP WITH HIGHLY DEVELOPED SKILLS WITHIN THREE-DIMENSIONAL WEAVING.

right: A heddle is an integral part of a loom. Each thread in the warp passes through a heddle, which is used to separate the warp threads for the passage of the weft. Each heddle has an eye in the center through which the warp is threaded.

IRIS HANTVERK
BRUSH MAKER

A SWEDISH INITIATIVE TO HELP VISUALLY IMPAIRED PEOPLE INTO WORK, IRIS HANTVERK CREATES BEAUTIFUL, TACTILE BRUSHES FOR A WIDE RANGE OF HOUSEHOLD USES.

Expertly merging Scandinavian design with an earthy functionality, Iris Hantverk is a Swedish brush manufacturer based in Enskede, a southern suburb of Stockholm. Their brushes are made by hand from natural materials for everyday household uses and include bath, nail, kitchen, and cleaning brushes alongside brooms, dustpans, and boot scrapers. Recently taken over by a young couple, Rikard Sparrenhök and Sara Edhäll, the brushes are designed by a collective of designers and produced in-house by blind craftsmen. "Both Rikard and I have held various tasks in the company over the years—to grow and develop with a company motivates you to stay," says Sara. "Another reason is all our colleagues and the former CEO, there has always been a spirit of openness and the ability to influence your work. We manufacture products that we are proud to work with."

Iris Hantverk shares a lot of its history with the visually impaired organization in Sweden that was founded in 1870 by Dr. Axel Beskov at the Manilla School in Stockholm—a workhouse for impaired craftsmen. In 1889, a group of workmen from the Manilla School founded the politically independent organization, De Blindas Förening [The Society for the Blind] whose purpose it was to encourage visually impaired

people to participate actively in social environments such as musical events and lectures, but primarily to integrate them into the workforce by offering support for equal access to employment. In 1906, the society acquired a building for the purpose of further aiding the craftsmen. It would serve a number of functions— office and library, a warehouse for raw materials, the brush binding factory, and a shop. This undertaking became the foundation of what Iris Hantverk is today.

THE CONSTRUCTION OF A HANDMADE BRUSH STARTS WITH A PIECE OF WOOD THAT THE CRAFTSMEN SAW, MILL, AND SAND TO ACHIEVE THE DESIRED SHAPE AND SMOOTHNESS.

Working with materials such as Sri Lankan bassine, coconut fiber, goat and horse hair, pig bristle and Mexican white fiber, the construction of a handmade brush starts with a piece of wood that the craftsmen saw, mill, and sand to achieve the desired shape and smoothness. Either lacquered or oiled, the wood is then drilled with holes for the bundles of bristles. The holes are made small on the top of the brush and

then widened so that they are larger on the other side where the bristles come out, with a regular vegetable brush having about forty holes and a tailor's brush having as many as 255 filled with bristle. Each individual bundle of bristles is attached by a wire with the help of a hook, normally a stainless steel wire, which is pulled into a loop through the narrowest end of the hole towards the wide end. The hook is attached to a ring around the craftsman's finger and each individual bundle of bristles is placed in the wire loop and pulled through. The bundle of bristles is picked by hand from a larger bale of material and when all the holes are filled, the brush is cut to the desired length and hackled to get it even with a cutting machine. Since the whole process is done by hand, the craftsmen rely fully on their hands in order to "see" what they are doing, tracing the smoothness of the wood or the placement of the bristles with their fingertips. "The brushes are made by visually impaired craftsmen," Sara adds. "It's an old tradition in Sweden that visually impaired craftsmen ribbon brushes. Because their sight is impaired it reinforces other senses such as touch, which means that their sight is not necessary to bind a brush; however, one does not become a skillful brushmaker without a feeling for the craft. It makes no difference if it is a visually, impaired craftsman who binds the bristles in terms of the appearance and quality of the product, but for us it is very important to preserve this profession for visually impaired people today, one of just a few career options."

Bringing another layer of meaning to the concept of sensitively made by hand, it is the company's long-term and inherent commitment to supporting the visually impaired that puts it at the forefront of social innovation and craftsmanship. What could be perceived as a weakness, its workforce, is turned into a strength (both socially and in terms of the finished item), resulting in a product that is palpably more tactile and meaningful in its physicality. •

BRINGING ANOTHER LAYER
OF MEANING TO THE CONCEPT
OF SENSITIVELY MADE BY
HAND, IT IS THE COMPANY'S
LONG-TERM AND INHERENT
COMMITMENT TO SUPPORTING
THE VISUALLY IMPAIRED
THAT PUTS IT AT THE FORE-
FRONT OF SOCIAL INNOVATION
AND CRAFTSMANSHIP.

left: When all the holes are filled with
bristles, the brush is cut and
hackeled for it to be even and smooth.

First, a piece of wood is sawed,
milled, and sanded, and then
holes for the bundle of bristles are
drilled. Individual bundles of
bristles are subsequently attached
to the base of the holes.

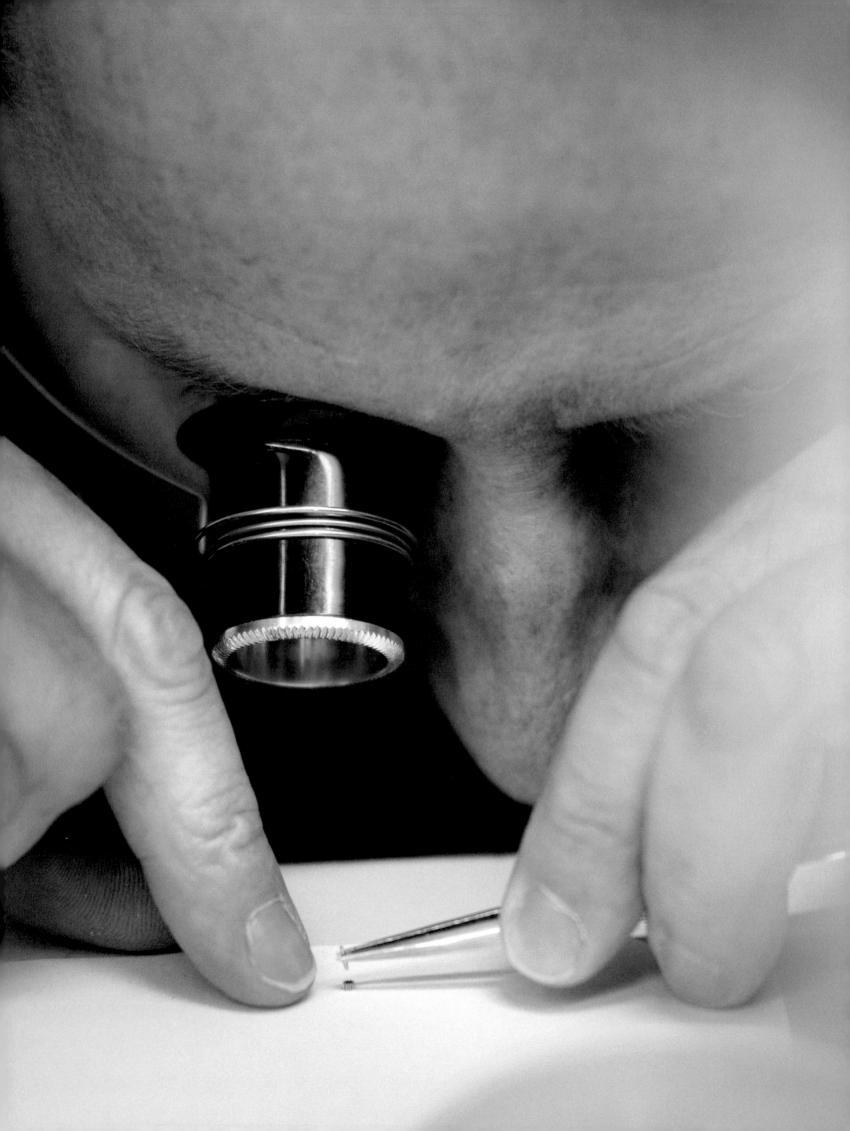

KARI VOUTILAINEN
WATCHMAKER

FINNISH-BORN KARI VOUTILAINEN IS ONE OF THE WORLD'S LEADING INDEPENDENT WATCHMAKERS, WORKING FROM HIS SWISS WORKSHOP TO CREATE AN EXTREMELY LIMITED NUMBER OF ASTONISHING TIMEPIECES, EACH ONE CRAFTED BY HAND.

In the tiny municipality of Môtiers, in the Neuchâtel region of western Switzerland, master watchmaker Kari Voutilainen produces some of the most influential timepieces in contemporary watchmaking today. With an output of only 40 to 50 watches per year (Rolex produces in the region of 2,000 per day), Kari and his team of just 15 watchmakers have caused something of a stir in recent years in the famously closed world of fine watchmaking. Originally from Finland, Kari entered a Finnish watchmaking school at the age of 22, before moving to Switzerland to perfect his craft. After a spell at Parmigiani, under the master watchmaker Charles Meylan, where he spent time restoring some of the world's rarest and most complicated antique watches and clocks, Kari spent some time passing on his knowledge as the head of the Swiss school he attended before finally founding Voutilainen in 2002 and showing at the international watch fair in Basel for the first time in 2005.

A deep understanding of intricate complications and antique watch restoration was an invaluable foundation for Kari, who has taken this knowledge and used it to push technological boundaries in his watches to the delight of the establishment, winning the prestigious Grand Prix de Genève in 2007. The concept of "in-house" production is something that watch-buying customers at the highest level consider to be very important. Beyond the pedigree of a name, it's the ability of a house to produce all the internal components required for a complete watch that really gets people excited. For brands belonging to luxury groups with enormous resources at their disposal, this can mean simply acquiring existing case and movement makers and relabeling them for the market, but for Voutilainen obviously this wasn't an option. Today almost every component that goes to make up a Voutilainen watch is produced by hand in his workshop, an incredible feat for such a small manufacturers.

THE AMOUNT OF TIME IT CAN TAKE TO PRODUCE A SINGLE PIECE IS ASTONISHING, AND THIS IS SOMETHING THAT SETS VOUTILAINEN WATCHES AS FAR APART AS IT'S POSSIBLE TO BE FROM THE CONCEPT OF "MASS-MARKET LUXURY."

With a particular emphasis on decoration and finishing, the Voutilainen aesthetic is refined and unostentatious despite its fine detailing. Dials are engine turned by hand on antique lathes to create the hypnotic guilloché motifs that have become a signature of the house. When the demand for Voutilainen timepieces far outstrips supply, Kari is well aware of the burdens on his time, but feels strongly that he has to continue to pick up his tools and connect with the craft that he loves. "There is an ever-lurking danger

Watchmaker Kari Voutilainen has devoted himself to developing the ultimate new and unique watch mechanism.

left: Tourbillion and Zodiac wristwatches.

that you become a manager and are never behind the bench anymore," he says. "The product will suffer with that, and within the shortest time, you have sold your soul to the devil. This is why, from the very beginning of starting for myself I defined exactly what my goals were, which timepieces I wanted to create in the future, how much time I was willing to spend on non-watchmaking activities like organization and the like." The amount of time it can take to produce a single piece is astonishing (up to 2,000 hours in some cases), and this is something that sets Voutilainen watches as far apart as it's possible to be from the concept of "mass-market luxury."

In an era of "more is more" haute horology, where competing brands in an increasingly saturated market strive to build ever more outrageous creations in order to grab headlines as well as customers, there is something inspiring about both the work and the ethos of Kari and his team. Concentrating on a discreet form of quiet luxury, they are creating remarkable timepieces with a respect for the past that will have people talking about them well into the future. •

MASARU OKUYAMA
SHOEMAKER

DISSATISFIED WITH THE DIRECTION OF HIS COMFORTABLE BUT ULTIMATELY UNFULFILLING LIFE, MASARU OKUYAMA SET OUT TO PURSUE A PERSONAL DREAM OF BECOMING A BESPOKE SHOEMAKER. TODAY HE RUNS A WORKSHOP IN HONG KONG, CREATING REFINED, ELEGANT SHOES FROM THE FINEST NATURAL MATERIALS.

After graduating from Nihon University College of Art, Masaru Okuyama began working for a Japanese jewelry brand, but despite the good salary and a comfortable life, he felt something fundamental was missing. That's when he decided to become a shoemaker. After an intensive two-year program at a Japanese shoemaking school and an apprenticeship under master craftsman Chihiro Yamaguchi, he set up his own business in 2008 focusing on bespoke shoemaking, with a belief that "A pair of shoes is the attire that expresses your seriousness about life."

Like all great creatives, he experienced moments of doubt on his journey, even traveling to Paris to try and secure an apprenticeship with one of the renowned European shoemaking houses. After a series of disheartening rebuttals, a chance encounter with shoemaker Ricardo Bestetti in Milan led him to his current path. Bestetti reassured him that as a fully trained shoemaker, Okuyama could create a bespoke pair of shoes entirely from scratch—from taking the customer's measurements to creating the last, and then crafting the shoe and polishing it to completion. If he trained with one of the more established names, he would become an expert at one stage of the process, but lose the rest of his accumulated knowledge.

After moving to Hong Kong, Masaru started working from the balcony of his apartment, and through referrals and word-of-mouth recommendations, his bespoke business was born. Today he has two apprentices under him and they work solely on bespoke shoes, a painstaking method that isn't for the faint of heart. The entire process, from taking measurements and choosing materials, making the lasts, checking the fit and designing a trial pair, making adjustments for comfort (often several times), then making and delivering the shoes can take from six months to a year. Working like a sculptor to create the perfect last for each foot, he is inspired by the curves of nature, noting that there are no straight lines on a shoe. "The design of shoes is all about curves," he says. "Lasts are like sculptures made for your feet.

Bespoke shoemaker
Masaru Okuyama.

MASARU OKUYAMA

HIS SHOES ARE CONSTRUCTED
ENTIRELY FROM LEATHER,
WITH THE SOLES USING
TRADITIONAL ENGLISH AND
GERMAN OAK BARK TANNED
COWHIDES WHICH THEMSELVES
TAKE AROUND 12 MONTHS TO
PREPARE FOR USE.

left: Semi brogue, black French box
calf, beveled waist shoe.

above: Masaru Okuyama uses a
wide variety of leathers for his
bespoke shoes, including sheep, goat,
cordovan, lizard, alligator,
lama, and shark, to name a few.

Even when there's a straight line in the design, it becomes a curve when it's on the last." His shoes are constructed entirely from leather (with occasional rubber soles on request for the wet Hong Kong cli-

MASARU'S WORK FEATURES A STRONG TRADITIONAL INFLUENCE, WITH SMALL, ALMOST IMPERCEPTIBLY PLAYFUL DETAILS.

mate), with the soles using traditional English and German oak bark tanned cowhides which themselves take around 12 months to prepare for use. When it comes to the upper of the shoes, the options are almost endless. While French box calf leather is the material he uses the most, Masaru has also been known to create shoes in sheep, goat, lizard, ostrich, alligator, and even shark leathers. Usually a single cowhide can provide the material for four to five pairs

of shoes, but Masaru prefers to make only a single pair from each hide, ensuring his shoes are constructed from only the finest part of the hide. He notes that each individual hide has its own characteristics, a personality even, and when cutting it and molding it to the shoe shape, it's very important to understand this character to bring out the best of the leather and create a shoe that is both beautiful and durable.

Striving to combine the stylish elegance beloved of French shoemakers, with the simplicity and dignity of the refined English aesthetic, Masaru's work features a strong traditional influence, with small, almost imperceptibly playful details like brogueing around the top of the shoe's tongue, creating shoes that are at once classical and contemporary. While one day he may seek to create a second line of custom-made shoes at a more accessible level, and even a ready-to-wear collection, the most important consideration for Masaru is that he can continue to craft shoes using his own hands, honing his skills, and further mastering his chosen vocation. •

above: Masaru Okuyama shoes combine meticulous Japanese savoir-faire with French elegance and a refined English aesthetic.

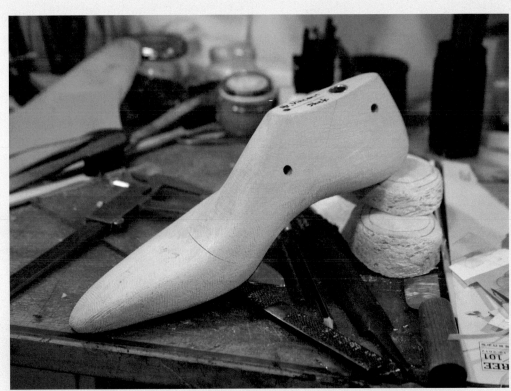

NIC WEBB
SPOON CARVER & CERAMICIST

WITH AN UNUSUALLY SENSITIVE APPROACH TO HIS WORK, THE POTTER AND SPOON CARVER NIC WEBB ALLOWS THE NATURAL BEAUTY OF THE MATERIALS TO SHINE THROUGH IN HIS BEGUILING CRAFTSMANSHIP.

Working principally with wood, but also incorporating stone, metal, ceramic, and paint into his work, Nic Webb is an artist-maker who embodies the notion of ancient crafts celebrated in a truly modern way. From his studio in South London, he creates "objects of art, design, function, and ornament" which subtly tread the line between the beautiful and practical. After graduating from Brighton University in 1994, he began to pursue spoon and woodcarving, techniques which are as old as civilization itself.

Nic uses greenwood (unseasoned wood), mainly from deciduous forests in the UK, particularly Suffolk where he spent his childhood. The beauty of this natural material lies in its inherent unpredictability. Before wood is seasoned and dried, it will twist, warp, and change shape during and after the carving process. This has the effect that the finished appearance is not determined only by Nic, but also by the wood itself. Many of the tools he uses today belonged to his great-great-grandfather, a carpenter who worked in Devon in the 19th century. By continuing to use these tools in his work, Nic is afforded not only the ability to explore techniques that are as relevant today as they would have been a century ago, but also to forge a significant connection to his own family heritage. The objects he creates are at once ancient and strikingly contemporary in their appearance, with the natural character of the wood being allowed to resonate in the final pieces, creating a tactile allure that begs the user to pick them up and to connect with the material.

In his ceramic work, Nic has embraced a similar sensibility and respect for the materials that he applies in his woodcarving. He sources his own clay, often from underneath the trees from which he has gathered wood for his spoons and bowls. "When you dig and prepare your own clay you may only produce a small amount with which to work," he says. "It brings a great sense of value to the material and careful consideration in the making." The ceramic works themselves employ primitive techniques to create vessels, which are at once delicate and functional. To glaze the ceramics, Nic uses the ancient Japanese technique of *nuka* or wood ash glazing. Using the scraps of greenwood from his woodcarving, the ceramics are bisque fired, before the ash is collected, washed, and prepared to make the glaze. Because trees draw in minerals including silica from the soil through their roots, when the wood is burned, the organic matter is removed and only the silica remains. When this silica is heated to a very high temperature, it melts to become glass, which can be used to glaze the ceramic creating an ephemeral and unexpected finish.

Although it's not a stipulation, there is every chance that the glaze on a pot may be derived from the ash of a tree that grew in the clay that the pot itself is crafted from. The cyclical nature of these natural connections is very important to Nic's creative process. This unique synergy of craft, material, and the natural elements involved in his methodology sets Nic apart as a craftsman in the truest sense of the word. •

Nic Webb in his
South London workshop.

above: Stoneware bowl with
Nuka glaze and Holly spoon.
Various wooden spoons.

right: Stoneware vessel with silver
spoon and black oak handle.

"WHEN YOU DIG AND PREPARE
YOUR OWN CLAY YOU MAY ONLY
PRODUCE A SMALL AMOUNT
WITH WHICH TO WORK.
IT BRINGS A GREAT SENSE OF
VALUE TO THE MATERIAL AND
CAREFUL CONSIDERATION IN
THE MAKING."

NORTON & SONS
TAILOR

A VENERATED GENTLEMEN'S SPORTING TAILOR,

NORTON & SONS HAD FALLEN OFF THE MAP WHEN PATRICK GRANT

RESTORED THE HOUSE TO ITS FORMER GLORY IN 2005.

Norton & Sons was established in 1821 by Walter Norton as a tailor to the "Gentlemen of the City of London." It was originally located on the Strand but moved to Savile Row in the 1860s to join the ranks of tailors in what was to become the epicenter and home of British bespoke tailoring. After having worked many years as an engineer, Patrick Grant spotted a "business for sale" advertisement in the *Financial Times* and bought the company in 2005 after having sold his house, his car, borrowing from a bank, and raising money from a group of friends.

One of the oldest tailors on Savile Row, located in number 16 on the east side of the street, Norton & Sons soon gained a reputation as a sporting tailor amongst "rugged and robust gentlemen" for its immaculately cut suits and garments. The choice for both Lord Carnarvon when he discovered Tutankhamon's tomb and Henry Stanley when he presumed to have found Dr Livingstone further enhanced this reputation, with the house also tailoring suits for members of the royal households of Austria, Belgium, Denmark, Italy, Prussia, Spain, Portugal, and the United Kingdom, three US Presidents as well as Winston Churchill.

NORTON & SONS GAINED A REPUTATION AS A SPORTING TAILOR AMONGST "RUGGED AND ROBUST GENTLEMEN" FOR ITS IMMACULATELY CUT SUITS AND GARMENTS.

Bespoke suit making starts with the client visiting his tailor and getting measured for his own personal pattern, in order to create a proportionate and balanced silhouette and a flattering line. This pattern is then refined through the fitting process—for a new customer this process will take approximately three to four months and involve three to four fittings. Sourcing predominantly British cloths, using worsteds from mills in Yorkshire, flannels from the west of England, woolen spun tweeds from the Borders, Yorkshire, the Highlands and the islands of Harris, Mull, and Islay, Norton & Sons offers a choice of 8000 cloth patterns, from 6 1/2 oz to 32 oz in weight, and from Super 100s grade to Super 250s, cashmere, and vicuña which Patrick can advise yout on. Every lounge suit, overcoat, blazer, sports jacket, vest, trousers, dinner suit, smoking jacket, dress coat,

Norton & Sons creative director and fashion designer Patrick Grant.

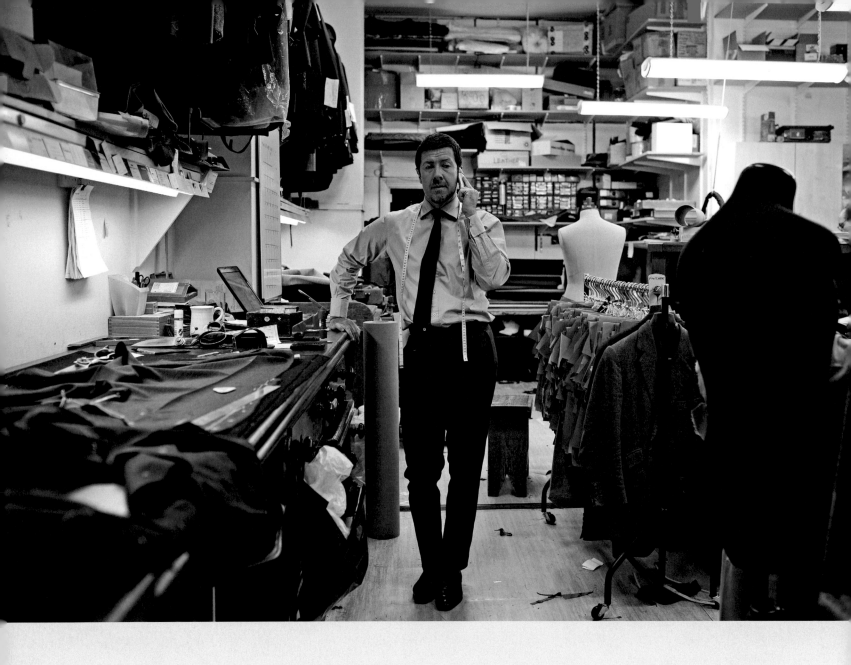

or morning coat, not to mention the sports offerings, are cut and fitted under the watchful eye of head cutter Stephen Allen. He favors a simple, classically cut garment with a shaped waist and neat structured shoulder that gives for a well-balanced and perfectly proportioned look. Everything, without compromise, is stitched and assembled by hand. Grant explains, "Every customer has their own pattern, hand cut to his individual measurements and figure, refined through the fitting process. Our tailoring team is comprised of the finest specialist coat-makers, vest-makers, trouser-makers and finishing tailors, trained in their art on Savile Row. The making of a single suit can involve up to 11 craftsmen, up to 60 hours of work, and will take many weeks to complete." Today, Norton & Sons make about 300 suits a year. Since taking over the company, Patrick Grant has gone on to expand its presence beyond the hallowed doors of Savile Row. He also re-launched the then defunct

above: The Norton & Sons atelier.

right: View of the Norton & Sons storefront at 16 Savile Row in London's Mayfair district.

Norton & Sons subsidiary E. Tautz as a ready-to-wear brand in 2009 and in recognition, was awarded the Menswear Designer of the Year in 2010 at the British

THE MAKING OF A SINGLE SUIT CAN INVOLVE UP TO 11 CRAFTSMEN, UP TO 60 HOURS OF WORK, AND WILL TAKE MANY WEEKS TO COMPLETE.

Fashion Awards and is now working on venturing into womenswear. In 2013, he partnered with English high-street department store Debenhams launching Hammond & Co, a Savile Row inspired collection as well as consulting for Barbour, Alexander McQueen, and Kim Jones. The many different strings to Patrick's bow all balance and help each business to grow, moving towards a modern rejuvenation, while retaining a sense of integrity and quality at their core. •

NORTON & SONS

ESTD. 1821.

left: Autographed picture from
Frank Sinatra to Norton & Sons
head cutter Stephen Allen
dating back to 1980:
"For Stephen—You make a
great shirt! My very best to you."

right: Classic lines and fitted,
clean cuts define the Norton & Sons
aesthetic.

Index

KAIKADO Kyoto, Japan
www.kaikado.jp p. 10
Photos: Kaikado

KARI VOUTILAINEN Môtiers, Switzerland
www.voutilainen.ch pp. 250-253
Photos: Kari Voutilainen

KLAR SEIFEN Heidelberg, Germany
www.klarseifen.de pp. 56-59
Photos: Christiane Bach/Klar Seifen

LABOUR & WAIT London, United Kingdom
www.labourandwait.co.uk p. 17
Photos: Andrew Moran, Flora Deborah p. 17 left, top right

LAPICIDA London, United Kingdom
www.lapicida.com p. 7
Photos: Lapicida p. 7 top left, bottom left

LIVERANO & LIVERANO Florence, Italy
www.liverano.com pp. 206-209
Photos: Elliot Hammer

LLADRÓ Valencia, Spain
www.lladro.com p. 11
Photos: Francisco Gimeno, Lladró p. 11 top right, bottom right

LOBMEYR Vienna, Austria
www.lobmeyr.at pp. 124-131
Photos: Lobmeyr

MASARU OKUYAMA Hong Kong, China
www.masaruokuyama.com pp. 254-259
Photos: Masaru Okuyama

MAST BROTHERS Brooklyn, NY, USA
www.mastbrothers.com pp. 154-157
Photos: Gentl & Hyers p. 154, 156 top left / Mindy Best p. 156 bottom / Mast Brothers p. 155, 156 top right, 157

MICHAEL RUH London, United Kingdom
www.michaelruh.com p. 13
Photos: Peter Holmboe, Michael Ruh Studio p. 13 bottom two left

MOYNAT Paris, France
www.moynat.com pp. 210-215
Photos: Paul Gruber, Moynat Paris

MÜHLBAUER Vienna, Austria
www.muehlbauer.at pp. 158-163
Photos: Mühlbauer p. 9 third from top, right column

NAKAGAWA MOKKOUGEI Kyoto, Japan
www.nakagawa-mokkougei.com pp. 72-75
Photos: Shuji Nakagawa p. 9 second from top, right column

NIC WEBB London, United Kingdom
www.nicwebb.com pp. 260-263
Photos: Nic Webb p. 9 fourth from top, p. 263 bottom / Jesse Mewburn p. 260 / Tif Hunter p. 261, 262

NORTON & SONS London, United Kingdom
www.nortonandsons.co.uk pp. 264-269
Photos: Nicholas Andrews, Maximiliano Braun / Reportage by Getty Images p. 8 bottom

PORZELLAN MANUFAKTUR NYMPHENBURG München, Germany
www.nymphenburg.com pp. 226-233
Photos: Porzellan Manufaktur Nymphenburg p. 9 first from top, right column

ORGELBAU KLAIS Bonn, Germany
www.orgelbau-klais.com pp. 60-65
Photos: Sascha Müller Jäntsch p. 8 second from top / Klais p. 61 / Antonio Ceruelo p. 62 / Boris Schafgans p. 63 top / Andri Schmidt p. 63 bottom, p. 65 top left, p. 65 bottom two / Ivo Mayr p. 65 top right / Oliver Hartman p. 64 top / Mitte Guteridge p. 54 bottom

PIERRE FREY Paris, France
www.pierrefrey.com pp. 146-153
Photos: Louis Sommer, Antony Dorfmann, Dorothée Demey, Pierre Frey

RALEIGH DENIM WORKSHOP Raleigh, NC, USA
www.raleighworkshop.com pp. 108-111
Photos: Nick Pironio

RAW-EDGES, YAEL MER & SHAY ALKALAY London, United Kingdom
www.raw-edges.com pp. 14-15
Photos: Joel Tettamanti, Raw-Edges p. 9 bottom left, p. 15 top two

RENÉ TALMON L'ARMÉE Paris, France/Berlin, Germany
www.renetalmonlarmee.com p. 13
Photos: René Talmon l'Armée p. 8 top, p. 13 bottom right

SANTA MARIA NOVELLA Florence, Italy
www.santamarianovellausa.com p. 7
Photos Property of Officina Profumo - Farmaceutica di Santa Maria Novella, Katy Rose p. 7 right top, right bottom

SHINOLA Detroit, USA
www.shinola.com pp. 132-141
Photos: Shinola p. 8 fourth from top, right

STÄHLEMÜHLE Eigeltingen, Germany
www.staehlemuehle.de pp. 188-197
Photos: Stählemühle, Bernd Kammerer p. 188, 191, 193, 194 / Christoph Keller p. 189, 190, 196, 197 bottom, p. 197 / Ingmar Kurth p. 190 top, p. 192 top / e15 p. 192 bottom

THE HOME PROJECT DESIGN STUDIO Berlin, Germany
www.the-home-project.com p. 18-19
Photos: Janina Wick p. 18, p. 19 middle left, bottom right / The Home Project Design Studio, p. 19 top, bottom left, Graphics: Joana and Mariana

THE NEW CRAFTSMEN London, United Kingdom
www.thenewcraftsmen.com p. 16
Photos: The New Craftsmen, p. 17 top left, bottom right

THERESIENTHAL Zwiesel, Germany
www.theresienthal.de p. 11
Photos: Tina Ditz, David Aussehofer p. 11 top, middle and bottom left

WALT SIEGL MOTORCYCLES Harrisville, NH, USA
www.waltsiegl.com pp. 12-13
Photos: Brian P. O'Neil, Michael Rubenstein p. 12, p. 13 top

WEDNESDAY PAPER WORKS Berlin, Germany
www.wednesday-paper-works.com pp. 182-187
Photos: Ursula Paletta, Wednesday Paper Works

The CRAFT and the MAKERS

TRADITION WITH ATTITUDE

This book was conceived,
edited, and designed by Gestalten.

Edited by Duncan Campbell, Charlotte Rey,
Sven Ehmann, and Robert Klanten

Introduction and profiles by
Duncan Campbell and Charlotte Rey
Additional research by Marie le Fort
Additional texts by Noelia Hobeika and
Vanessa Obrecht

Layout, design, and cover by Andrè M. Wyst
Cover photography by Achim Hatzius
Typefaces: Belwe™ by Bitstream,
Garamond by Claude Garamond
Proofreading by transparent Language Solutions

Printed by Optimal Media GmbH,
Röbel/Müritz
Made in Germany

Published by Gestalten, Berlin 2014
ISBN: 978-3-89955-548-6
2nd printing, 2015

© Die Gestalten Verlag GmbH & Co. KG. Berlin 2014
All rights reserved. No part of this publication may be reproduced
or transmitted in any form or by any means, electronic or
mechanical, including photocopy or any storage and retrieval
system, without permission in writing from the publisher.

Respect copyrights, encourage creativity!
For more information, please visit www.gestalten.com.

Bibliographic information published by the
Deutsche Nationalbibliothek.
The Deutsche Nationalbibliothek lists this publication in the
Deutsche Nationalbibliografie; detailed bibliographic data are
available online at http://dnb.d-nb.de

None of the content in this book was published in exchange for
payment by commercial parties or designers; Gestalten selected all
included work based solely on its artistic merit.

This book was printed on paper certified by the FSC®.